MAKING MANDALAS

27 crochet designs to get your hooks into

UK Terms

Emily Littlefair

Copyright © 2023 by Emily Littlefair.

All rights reserved. My patterns and tutorials are for your personal use only,
are my property and are protected by copyright.

No part of this book, text, or photographs or illustrations may be reproduced or transmitted in any form by any means by print, electronic, photocopying, video, internet or in any way known or as yet unknown, or stored in a retrieval system, without written permission obtained beforehand from the author.

Technical Editing by Emily Reiter

Printed by IngramSpark

First edition 2023

Published by Emily Penn

Paperback ISBN: 978-0-6457877-1-9
Hardcover ISBN: 978-0-6457877-5-7

DEDICATION

This book is dedicated to my boys, everything I do is for you.
You will never know how much I love you.
Thank you for being the best gift I have ever received.

In the spirit of reconciliation, I respectfully acknowledge the Traditional Custodians of country throughout Australia and their connections to land, sea and community.
I pay my respects to their Elders past and present and extend that respect to all Aboriginal and Torres Strait Islander people.

ACKNOWLEDGEMENTS

This endeavour would not have been possible without the love and support from Richard, my husband. For letting me get lost in hours of designing, yarn and mandalas EVERY-WHERE, impromptu photoshoots, and for all the hours it has taken to put it all together into an actual book and all the time it took for me to learn how to do it all myself. For his understanding when sometimes it felt like I bit off more than I could chew. For being there through all the highs and lows and for taking me as the crazy crochet lady that I am. I look foward to spending weekends with you and the boys again. Hopefully you haven't forgotten who I am haha.

Words cannot express my gratitude to my amazing team of testers. This has been a feat I could not have achieved without you. You are my rocks, my many sets of extra keen eyes, vigilant hooks and hands and even though we all live around the world, we're forever connected by our special bond. In no particular order, I praise Margaret Richards, Audrey Muller, Mirjam Annaars, Lyn Merton, Natasha Ireland, Krystle Patrono, Narelle Mitchell, Kathy Mant, Antoinette Loggenberg, Melissa Pearce, Melissa Coles, Silke Spit, Natalie Rowland, Jane Reid, Amanda, Renée Roy, Ruth Bracey, Susan Marcille, Kim Siebenhausen, Tracey Whiting and Paulina Smith Maraboli.

I could not have undertaken this journey without Shelley Husband and her guidance and help throughout this entire process. Thank you for your reassurance when I suffered self-doubt, was at the low-points, and couldn't see the end in sight. Even though this has been

such a learning curve, this would not have been possible without you. I would have thrown the towel in a long time ago.

I am also so grateful for my dear friend Joy. Like Shelley, you were there to hear me whinge, share in the excitement when I had something new to share, such as another update with my process throughout the entire self-publishing journey and be there to pick me up and assure me that I was on the right path and to listen to my heart. I love that crochet has brought you into my life.

I would like to extend my sincere thanks to the rest of my family, for your continued support and encouragement. I hope to do you proud each and every day and also by constantly showing you what I am capable of because of what you have instilled within me.

Special thanks goes to Emily Reiter, my amazing tech-editor. For your sharp eyes and drive to be the best that you can be. I am looking forward to working with you in the future on many books and other patterns to come. I promise that next time, I will not give you all the patterns at once unless you are up for another challenge.

Last, but certainly not least, I would like to express my deepest appreciation to all of you who have supported me over the years by purchasing my patterns, sharing your makes (that makes my heart sing), commented on my social media posts and those who have shared in the memorable moments of completing workshops and retreats with me. Your continued support inspires me to continue designing and to be the best that I can be. Much love,

Em xxx

CONTENTS

WELCOME — 6

ABOUT ME — 8

COLOUR — 10

MANDALAS TO MAKE — 12

GLOSSARY — 134

HOOK COVERSION SIZES — 137

SYMBOLS & NOTES — 138

HOW TO INSERT BEADS — 139

STITCH KEY — 140

YARN USED — 141

HOOKS USED — 141

WELCOME

h e l l o

Oh my gosh! I did it! There were multiple times during the entire process where I thought of throwing in the towel, but it was at those moments, pushing through the darkness, when the light shone brightest.

KEEP IN THE LOOP

Follow me on Social Media and Website for all things Loopy Stitch.

Instagram	Facebook	Website

It does not matter how slowly you go as long as you do not stop.

~ CONFUCIUS ~

DESIGN NAMES

I chose to name my designs after virtues and morals, something that means a lot to me and how I live my life and would like to instil in my boys as they grow older.

I have also included their definitions which were sourced from dictionary.com.

Not only that but I tried my best to relate them to crochet for a little laugh and also a quote or saying as well. Little personal touches that I hope may spark that light inside you that you might have been looking for.

BEST WISHES

I really hope you enjoy making all the pieces in the book, some are small and do not take much time and others require a little more concentration.

Be mindful of your crochet time, enjoy it, soak it up, and be present in every moment.

I wish the crochet fairies find you at night to weave in your ends and find the missing hooks that the lounge takes without you even noticing. But most importantly...

...Happy Hooking! Much love,

Em xxx

COLOUR

It's no secret I love colour. It speaks to me.

It's the first thing I choose before I begin designing and I really believe the following quote.

Colour possesses a language without words.

BILLY DUGGER

ABOUT ME

Designer, Author, Photographer, Graphic Designer (all self-taught lol)

Emily

Hi there. My name is Emily and I love designing crochet patterns, especially mandala designs. I find something calming and mindful about working in rounds. They bring me so much joy.

This is my first self-published book and because I love learning and doing everything myself, it has definitely been a learning curve. Not knowing what to expect or how to do it, I do love a good challenge.

I have a favourite saying 'without challenge, we cannot grow' and boy have I grown whilst doing this book. But seriously, there were some days I just loved it, some where I would rather have forgotten about it altogether, but persistence of wanting to see these designs on your hooks were inspiration and motivation to keep going.

I am a mum to three active, beautiful, football-crazy boys who light up my life more than they will ever know. I need to keep my hands busy, to help with my overactive mind, so designs pour off my hooks and sometimes I cannot keep up and forget to write them down. Hindering my future self when I go to write them up for testing and publishing. I love nature and am grateful for all the beauty that surrounds me.

I am happily married to another football-crazy person. So during football (round ball/soccer) season and pre-season, our lives are crazy busy, but it seems our family thrives on it. So we just keep on doing it. Milo (dog) and Molly (cat) are also part of our lives and I can't imagine life without them.

ABUNDANCE
MANDALA

noun. an extremely plentiful or oversufficient quantity or supply
An abundance of yarn.

FINISHED SIZE
30cm/11.8in unblocked

MATERIALS

Naturals Organic Cotton
One ball of each

Colour 1 7168 Gypsum

Colour 2 7199 Deep Sea

Colour 3 7175 Citron

US G-6 / UK 8 / (4mm) hook

Yarn Needle

Scissors

Stitch Marker

NOTES & TIPS

Third Loop

Work in the loop behind the 'V' as stated.

Round 14

Do not make the chain stitches too tight or too loose in this round. If they are made too tight, they could cause the mandala to start cupping.

Back Loop Only

When making stitches into the back loop only, work into the third loop as well to secure it nicely.

You can never have too much yarn.

Round 1: C1

Make a MR, or (ch 5, join to first ch to form ring) beg tr3cl in ring, ch 3, (tr3cl, ch 3) five times in ring, join to first cl to form ring, fasten off. *<6 tr3cl, 6 ch-3 sp>*

Round 2: C2

In any cl, make a standing [fphtr around cl, 3 htr in ch-3 sp] around, join to first fphtr made, fasten off. *<6 fphtr, 18 htr>*

Round 3: C3

Blo htr in any fphtr, blo htr in same st, blo htr in next 3 sts, [2 blo htr in next st, blo htr in next 3 sts] around, join to first blo htr made, fasten off. *<30 blo htr>*

Round 4: C1 - *No st is skipped from Rnd 3 when fpdtr are made*

Dc in first st from prev round, fpdtr around cl from Rnd 1, [dc in next 5 sts, fpdtr around cl] around, on final repeat, dc in last 4 unworked sts, join to first dc made, fasten off. *<6 fpdtr, 30 dc>*

Round 5: C2

In any fpdtr, make a standing [pop in fpdtr, tr in next 2 sts, (tr, ch 1, tr) in next st, tr in next 2 sts] around, join to first pop made, fasten off. *<6 pop, 36 tr, 6 ch-1 sp>*

Round 6: C3

In any ch-1 sp, make a standing [(3 tr, ch 2, 3 tr) in ch-1 sp, sk 2 sts, dc in next st, fpdtr around fpdtr from Rnd 4, dc in pop, fpdtr around same fpdtr, dc in next st, sk 2 sts] around, join to first tr made, fasten off. *<36 tr, 6 ch-2 sp, 18 dc, 12 fpdtr>*

Round 7: C1

In fpdtr before pop, make a standing [fpdc around fpdtr before pop, 5 tr in dc, fpdc around next fpdtr, sk 2 sts, bphtr around next 2 sts, 3 htr in ch-2 sp (place marker in first htr made only), bphtr around next 2 sts, sk 2 sts] around, join to first fpdc made, fasten off. *<12 fpdc, 30 tr, 24 bphtr, 18 htr>*

Round 8: C2– *This round is worked in the 3rd loop*

In marked st, make a standing htr (place marker in st), htr in next 2 sts, ch 4, sk 4 sts, [htr in next 3 sts, ch 4, sk 4 sts] around, join to first htr made, fasten off. *<36 htr 3rd loop, 12 ch-4 sp>*

Round 9: C3

In marked st, make a standing tr in 3rd loop of st (place marker in st), tr in 3rd loop of next 2 sts, 5 tr in ch-4 sp, [tr in 3rd loop of next 3 sts, 5 tr in ch-4 sp] around, join to first tr made in 3rd loop, fasten off. *<60 tr, 36 blo tr>*

Round 10: C1

In first st from prev rnd, make a standing dc, [2 dc in next st, dc in next 7] around, on final repeat, omit last dc, join to first dc made, fasten off. *<108 dc>*

Round 11: C2

In first st from prev rnd, make a standing [tr, ch 1, sk st] around, join to first tr made, fasten off. *<54 tr, 54 ch-1 sp>*

Round 12: C3 - *Fold Rnd 11 to the back, this Rnd is worked into the unworked sts from Rnd 10.*

In first unworked st, make a standing [tr, ch 1 (place marker in first ch-1 sp only), sk st] around, join to first tr made, fasten off. *<54 tr, 54 ch-1 sp>*

Round 13: C1

Fphtr around any tr from Rnd 11 or 12, fphtr around each st from Rnds 11 & 12 around, join to first fphtr made, fasten off. *<108 fphtr>*

Round 14: C2 – *This Rnd is worked into Rnds 8 & 13, also note there are 4 unworked sts between sets of 5 dc*

Join with sl st to any first htr from Rnd 8, sl st in next 3 sts (the 4th st will be the first ch st in Rnd 8 after last htr), ch 7 (not too loose or tight), working into Rnd 13, dc directly into st aligned with last sl st just made, dc in next 4 sts in Rnd 13, ch 7 (not too loose or tight), [sl st to first htr of group from Rnd 8, sl st in next 3 sts, ch 7, dc in aligned Rnd 13 st from last sl st, dc in next 4 sts in Rnd 13, ch 7] around, join to first sl st, fasten off. *<48 sl st, 24 ch-7 sp, 60 dc>*

Round 15: C3 – *This rnd is worked into Rnds 12, 13 and 14.*

In marked ch-sp from Rnd 12, make a standing [htr in first ch-1, (htr in next st, htr in ch-1 sp) two times, pick up 3rd loop (bump) from first ch st of ch-7 made in prev rnd, make dc into unworked fphtr in Rnd 13, dc in next 2 sts, pick up 3rd loop (bump) of last ch st of ch-7 made in prev rnd and dc in next fphtr] around, join to first htr made, fasten off. *<48 dc, 60 htr>*

Round 16: C1

In last dc before htr in prev rnd, make a standing tr, tr in next 2 sts, [2 tr in next st, tr in next 8] around, on final repeat omit last 3 tr, join to first tr made, fasten off. *<120 tr>*

Round 17: C2

In first tr of 2 tr from prev rnd, make a standing tr, tr in next 2 sts, ch 3, sk 2 sts, [tr in next 3 sts, ch 3, sk 2 sts] around, join to first tr made, fasten off. *<72 tr, 24 ch-3 sp>*

Round 18: C3

In any middle tr, make a standing [pop in middle tr, ch 3, dc in ch-3 sp, ch 3] around, join to first pop, do not fasten off. *<24 pop, 48 ch-3 sp, 24 dc>*

Round 19: C3

Ch 1 (doesn't count as st), [(dc, ch 2, dc) in pop, 3 dc in ch-3 sp, fpdc around dc, 3 dc in ch-3 sp] around, join to first dc made, fasten off. *<192 dc, 24 ch-2 sp, 24 fpdc>*

Round 20: C1

[(Htr, ch 2, htr) in ch-2 sp, blo htr in next 2 sts, blo dc in next st, ch 1, sk st, fpdc around fpdc, ch 1, sk st, blo dc in next st, blo htr in next 2 sts] around, join to first htr made, fasten off. *<48 htr, 96 blo htr, 48 blo dc, 24 fpdc, 48 ch-1 sp, 24 ch-1 sp>*

ABUNDANCE
MANDALA

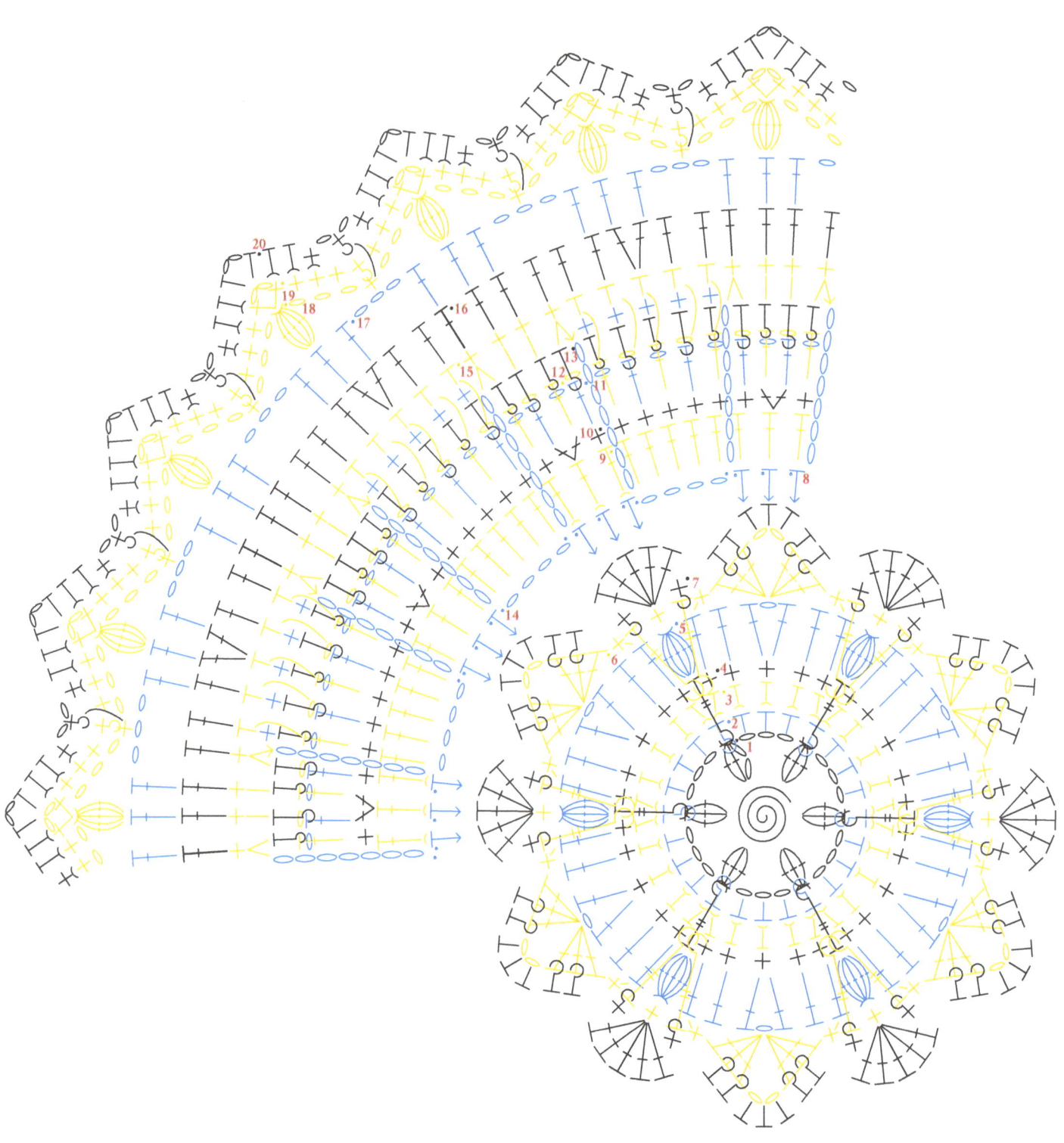

APPRECIATION
MANDALA

noun. gratitude; thankful recognition

The more I crochet, the more I have appreciation for what this magic wand and long stuff can turn into.

FINISHED SIZE
42cm/16.5in unblocked

MATERIALS

Special DK
One ball of each

Colour 1 1856 Dandelion
Colour 2 1711 Spice
Colour 3 1723 Tomato
Colour 4 1725 Sage

US 7 / UK 7 / (4.5mm) hook
Yarn Needle
Scissors
Stitch Marker/s
Ring is optional 50cm/19.7in used

NOTES & TIPS

Standing Stitches
If you are using different colours for each round, try to use standing stitches instead of starting chains.

Invisible Joins
These go hand in hand with Standing Stitches and hide the joins on each round.

Attaching to ring
Use stitch markers to attach your finished piece to the ring to see if it will fit nicely.

Trade your expectations for appreciation and your whole life will change.

Tony Robbins

Round 1: C1

Make a MR, or (ch 5, join to first ch to form ring), ch 3 (counts as tr), 15 tr in ring, join to top of ch 3, fasten off. *<16 tr>*

Round 2: C2

In any st, make a standing (tr + ch 1) in each st around, join to first tr made, fasten off. *<16 tr, 16 ch-1 sp>*

Round 3: C3

In any ch-1 sp, make a standing (tr2cl + ch 2) in each ch-1 sp around, join to first tr2cl made, fasten off. *<16 tr2cl, 16 ch-2 sp>*

Round 4: C4

In any cl, make a standing [fpdc around cl, dc in next ch-2 sp, fpdtr around tr from Rnd 2, dc in same ch-2 sp] around, join to first fpdc made, fasten off.

<16 fpdc, 16 fpdtr, 32 dc>

Round 5: C1

In any fpdtr, make a standing [pop in fpdtr, ch 2, sk st, dc in fpdc, ch 2, sk st] around, join to first pop made, fasten off.

<16 pop, 16 dc, 32 ch-2 sp>

Round 6: C – *This rnd may be slightly ruffled*

In any dc, make a standing [5 tr in dc, sk ch-2 sp, dc in pop, sk ch-2 sp] around, join to first tr made, fasten off. *<80 tr, 16 dc>*

Round 7: C3

Make a standing bptr around first tr of any 5-tr group, bptr around next 4 sts, sk dc, [bptr around next 5 tr, sk dc] around, join to first bptr, fasten off. *<80 bptr>*

Round 8: C4 – *Cl sts are made between sts, not in sts*

Make a standing [tr2cl in between first and last tr, ch 3, sk 2 sts, dc in next st (3rd tr), ch 3, sk 2 sts] around, join to first tr2cl made, fasten off. *<16 tr2cl, 16 dc, 32 ch-3 sp>*

Round 9: C1

Join with a [sl st to dc, (dc, htr, tr) in ch-3 sp, (tr, ch 2, tr) in cl, (tr, htr, dc) in ch-3 sp] around, join to first dc with sl st and fasten off. *<16 sl st, 32 dc, 32 htr, 64 tr, 16 ch-2 sp>*

Round 10: C2

In any ch-2 sp, make a standing [(dtr, ch 6, dtr) in ch-2 sp, ch 1] around, join to first dtr made, fasten off. *<32 dtr, 16 ch-6 sp, 16 ch-1 sp>*

Round 11: C3

In any ch-1 sp, make a standing [dc in ch-1 sp, dc in st, 7 dc in ch-6 sp, dc in st] around, join to first dc made, fasten off. *<160 dc>*

Round 12: C4

In first dc made prev rnd, make a standing [(dtr, ch 1) 4 times in dc, sk 4 sts, dc in next st, ch 1, sk 4 sts] around, join to first dtr made, fasten off. *<64 dtr, 16 dc, 80 ch-1 sp>*

Round 13: C1

After any dc, make a standing [(pop in ch-1 sp, ch 3, sk st) 4 times, pop in next ch-1 sp, ch 2] around, join to first pop made, fasten

off. <80 pop, 64 ch-3 sp, 16 ch-2 sp>

Round 14: C2

Make a standing [dc in ch-2 sp, sk pop, (2 dc, htr) in ch-3 sp, sk pop, (htr, 2 tr) in ch-3 sp, ch 2, sk pop, (2 tr, htr) in ch-3 sp, sk pop, (htr, 2 dc) in ch-3 sp, sk pop] around, join to first dc made, fasten off.

<80 dc, 64 htr, 64 tr, 16 ch-2 sp>

Round 15: C3

In first htr made in prev rnd, make a standing tr, tr in next 3 sts, (2 tr, ch 2, 2 tr) in ch-2 sp, tr in next 4 sts, sk 5 sts [tr in next 4 sts, (2 tr, ch 2, 2 tr) in ch-2 sp, tr in next 4 sts, sk 5 sts] around, join to first tr made, fasten off.

<192 tr, 16 ch-2 sp>

Round 16: C4

In any ch-2 sp, make a standing [(dc, ch 2, dc) in ch-2 sp, bphtr around next 5 sts, ch 1, sk 2 sts, bphtr around next 5 sts] around, join to first dc made, fasten off. <160 bphtr, 32 dc, 16 ch-2 sp>

APPRECIATION
MANDALA

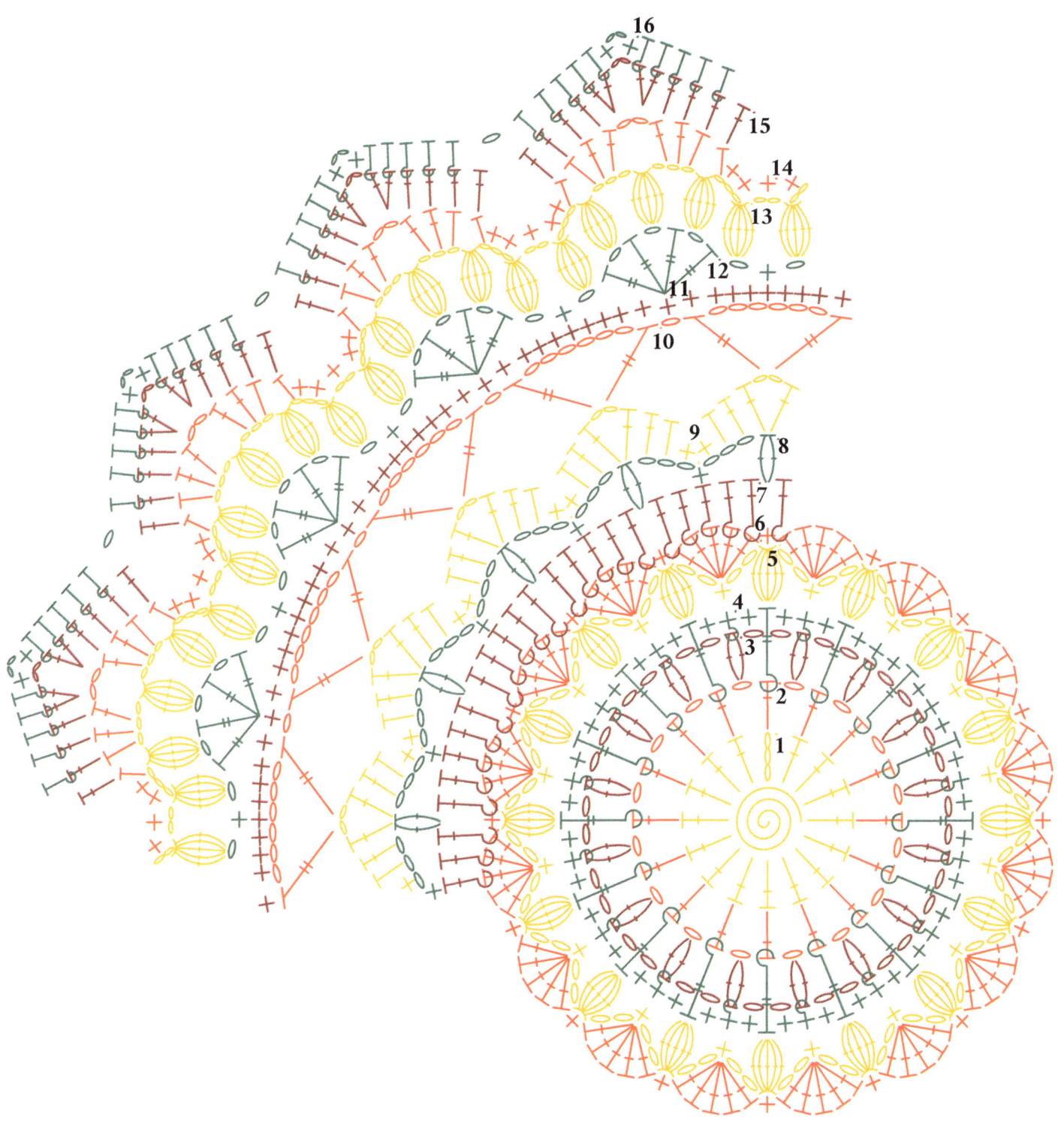

AWARENESS
MANDALA

noun. the state or condition of being aware; having knowledge; consciousness

Awareness of what crochet is capable of is truly amazing and inspiring

FINISHED SIZE

26.5cm/10.4in unblocked

MATERIALS

Naturals Organic Cotton
One ball of each

Colour 1 7199 Deep Sea
Colour 2 7168 Gypsum
Colour 3 7175 Citron

US G-6 / UK 8 / (4mm) hook
Yarn Needle
Scissors
Stitch Marker

NOTES & TIPS

Third Loop
Work in the loop behind the 'V' as stated.

Standing Stitches
If you are using different colours for each round, try to use standing stitches instead of starting chains.

Invisible Joins
These go hand in hand with Standing Stitches and hide the joins on each round.

Awareness is the greatest agent for change.

Eckhart Tolle

Round 1: C1

Make a MR, or (ch 4, join to first ch to form ring), ch 1, (doesn't count as st), 8 dc in ring, join to first dc made, do not fasten off. <8 dc>

Round 2: C1

Beg dtr3cl in same st as join, ch 3, (dtr3cl, ch 3) in each st around, join to first cl made, fasten off. <8 dtr3cl, 8 ch-3 sp>

Round 3: C2 – *Feel free to replace the standing dtr3cl with a beg dtr3cl if you prefer* [(dtr3cl, ch 3, dtr3cl) in ch-3 sp, ch 3, fptr around cl from Rnd 2, ch 3] around, join to first cl made, fasten off. <16 dtr3cl, 24 ch-3 sp, 8 fptr>

Round 4: C3

Make a standing [(2 dc, ch 2, 2 dc) in ch-3 point, dc in st, 2 dc in ch-3 sp, fpdc around fptr, 2 dc in ch-3 sp, dc in st] around, join to first dc made, fasten off. <80 dc, 8 fpdc, 8 ch-2 sp>

Round 5: C1

Make a standing [(htr, ch 2, htr), in ch-2 point, htr in 3rd loop next 5 sts, sl st in fpdc, htr in 3rd loop next 5 sts] around, join to first htr made, fasten off. <80 htr 3rd loop, 16 htr, 8 sl st, 8 ch-2 sp>

Round 6: C2 – *This round is worked in the 3rd loop except in the ch-2 point*

Make a standing [dc in ch-2 point, dc in next st, htr in next 2 sts, tr in next st, dtr2tog over next 5 sts skipping the 3 in middle, tr in next st, htr in next 2 sts, dc in next st] around, join to first dc made, fasten off. *<16 3rd loop dc, 32 3rd loop htr, 16 3rd loop tr, 8 3rd loop dtr2tog, 8 dc>*

Round 7: C2 – *Still using this colour and to hide the obvious join*

[Tr in dc, tr in next 4 sts, 2 tr in next st, tr in next 4 sts] around, join to first tr made, fasten off. *<88 tr>*

Round 8: C3

Make a standing dc in first tr from prev rnd, dc in next 5 sts, 2 dc in next st, [dc in next 10 sts, 2 dc in next st] around, on final repeat dc 4, join to first dc made, fasten off. *<96 dc>*

Round 9: C1

In second dc in Rnd 8, make a [pop in dc, ch 1, tr in 3rd loop next 2 sts] around, join to first pop made, fasten off. <32 pop, 32 ch-1 sp, 64 tr>

Round 10: C2 – *Start in a pop that aligns with the Rnd 5 point*

Make a standing (tr, ch 2, tr, ch 1) in each pop around, join to first tr made, fasten off. <64 tr, 32 ch-2 sp, 32 ch-1 sp>

Round 11: C2 – *This round is worked only in ch-2 sps*

Sl st to ch-2 sp, make a (beg dtr3cl, ch 3, dtr3cl) in same ch-2 sp, ch 3, dc in next ch-2 sp, ch 3, [(dtr3cl, ch 3, dtr3cl) in next ch-2 sp, ch 3, dc in next ch-2 sp, ch 3] around, join to

first cl made, fasten off. *<32 dtr3cl, 16 dc, 48 ch-3 sp>*

Round 12: C3

Make a standing [fpdc around dc from prev rnd, 3 dc in ch-3 sp, dc in st, (2 dc, ch 2, 2 dc) in ch-3 sp, dc in st, 3 dc in ch-3 sp] around, join to first fpdc made, fasten off. *<192 dc, 16 ch-2 sp, 16 fpdc>*

Round 13: C1

Make a standing [(dc, ch 2, dc) in ch-2 sp, dc 3rd loop in next 5 sts, sk st, sl st in fpdc, sk st, dc 3rd loop in next 5 sts] around, join to first dc made, fasten off. *<160 3rd loop dc, 32 dc, 16 ch-2 sp, 16 sl st>*

27

BALANCE
MANDALA

noun. a state of equilibrium or equipoise; equal distribution of weight, amount, etc.
Sometimes it's a hard job trying to find a balance between our wips, ufos and new projects.

FINISHED SIZE
42cm/16.5in unblocked

MATERIALS
Organic Cotton
One ball of each

Colour 1 7201 Indigo Wash
Colour 2 7198 Azure
Colour 3 7192 Sea Green
Colour 4 7191 Jade
Colour 5 7171 Leaf
Colour 6 7175 Citron

US G-6 / UK 8 / (4mm) hook
Yarn Needle
Scissors
Stitch Marker

NOTES & TIPS

Third Loop
Work in the loop behind the 'V' as stated.

Back Loop
When crocheting into the back loop, also pick up the third loop to keep it more secure.

Blocking
Feel free to give the chain loops a nice block after finishing.

Balance is not something you find, it's something you create.

Jana Kingsford

Round 1: C1

Make a MR, or (ch 5, join to first ch to form ring), ch 3 (counts as st), 15 tr in ring, join to top of ch 3, fasten off. *<16 tr>*

Round 2: C2

In any st, make a standing [(tr, ch 3, tr) in st, sk st] around, join to first tr made, fasten off. *<16 tr, 8 ch-3 sp>*

Round 3: C3

In ch-3 sp, make a standing [4 tr in ch-3 sp, fptr around next 2 sts as one] around, join to first tr made, fasten off. *<8 fptr, 32 tr>*

Round 4: C4

Around any fptr, make a standing [2 fptr around fptr, bptr around next 4 sts] around, join to first fptr made, fasten off. *<16 fptr, 32 bphtr>*

Round 5: C5

In between two fptr, make a standing [(tr, ch 4, tr) in between two fptr, ch 2, sk 3 sts, dc in between second and third bptr, ch 2, sk 3 sts] around, join to first tr made, fasten off. *<16 tr, 8 dc, 16 ch-2 sp, 8 ch-4 sp>*

Round 6: C6

Around any dc, make a standing [fpdc around dc, ch 1, sk ch-sp and st, (5 tr, ch 2, 5 tr) in ch-4 sp, ch 1, sk st and ch-sp] around, join to first fpdc made, fasten off. *<80 tr, 16 ch-2 sp, 8 fpdc>*

Round 7: C1 – *Place markers in ch-1 sps*

In any ch-2 point, make a standing [(2 dc, ch 1, 2 dc) in ch-2 point, dc in third loop next 3 sts, ch 7, sk 7 sts, dc in third loop of third tr and next 2 sts] around, join to first dc made, fasten off. *<32 dc, 48 third loop dc, 8 ch-1 sp, 8 ch-7 sp>*

Round 8: C2 – *Place markers in ch-1 sps*

In any ch-1 point, make a standing [(dc, ch 1, dc) in ch-1 point, dc in next 2 sts, ch 2, sk 3 sts, (pop, ch 2) four times in ch-7 sp, sk 3 sts, dc in next 2 sts] around, join to first dc made, fasten off. *<32 pop, 48 dc, 40 ch-2 sp, 8 ch-1 sp>*

Round 9: C3

In any ch-1 point, make a standing [dc in ch-1 point, ch 2, sk 3 sts, sk ch-sp, sk pop, (dtr, ch 2, dtr, ch 2) in each of the next 3 ch-2 sps, sk pop, sk ch-sp, sk 3 sts] around, join to first dc made, fasten off. *<48 dtr, 56 ch-2 sp, 8 dc>*

Round 10: C4

Around any dc, make a standing [fpdc around dc, (ch 2, sk ch-sp, bptr around st) three times, ch 1, (dtr, ch 3, dtr) in ch-2 sp, ch 1, (bptr around next st, ch 2, sk ch-sp) three times] around, join to first fpdc made, fasten off. *<48 bptr, 16 dtr, 48 ch-2 sp, 16 ch-1 sp, 8 fpdc, 8 ch-3 sp>*

Round 11: C5

In any fpdc, make a standing [(trtr2cl, ch 3, trtr2cl, ch 3, trtr2cl) in fpdc, ch 2, sk ch-sp, sk st, sk ch-sp, dc in bptr, ch 5, sk ch-sp, sk st, sk ch-sp, dc in dtr, (2 dc, ch 1, 2 dc) in ch-3

sp, dc in dtr, ch 5, sk ch-sp, sk st, sk ch-sp, dc in bptr, ch 2, sk ch-sp, sk st, sk ch-sp] around, join to first trtr2cl made, fasten off. *<24 trtr2cl, 64 dc, 16 ch-2 sp, 16 ch-5 sp, 16 ch-3sp>*

Round 12: C6

In any ch-1 point, make a standing [(tr, ch 3, tr) in ch-1 point, ch 3, sk 3 sts, dc in ch-5 sp, ch 2, sk st and ch-sp, dc in cl, ch 1, pop in ch-3 sp, ch 2, (fptr, ch 2, fptr) around cl, ch 2, pop in ch-3 sp, ch 1, dc in cl, ch 2, sk ch-sp and st, dc in ch-5 sp, ch 3, sk 3 sts] around, join to first tr made, fasten off. *<16 tr, 32 dc, 16 pop, 16 ch-1 sp, 32 ch-2 sp, 8 ch-2 point, 8 ch-3 point, 16 ch-3 sp, 16 fptr>*

Round 13: C1

In any ch-3 point, make a standing [(2 htr, ch 2, 2 htr) in ch-3 point, htr in st, 3 htr in ch-3 sp, htr in next st, sk ch-sp, htr in next st, htr in ch-sp, htr in pop, htr in ch-sp, htr in st, (2 htr, ch 2, 2 htr) in ch-2 point, htr in st, htr in ch-sp, htr in pop, htr in ch-sp, htr in st, sk ch-sp, htr in next st, 3 htr in ch-3 sp, htr in next st] around, join to first htr made, fasten off. *<224 htr>*

Rounds 14-17:

In any ch-2 point, make a standing [(htr, ch 2, htr) in ch-2 point, blo htr in next 6 sts, sk 2 sts, blo htr in next 6 sts] around, join to first htr made, fasten off. *<196 blo htr, 32 htr>*

Rnd 14 - C2
Rnd 15 - C3
Rnd 16 - C4
Rnd 17 - C5
Round 18: C6

In any ch-2 sp, make a standing [(dc, ch 8, dc) in ch-2 sp, blo dc in next 6 sts, sk 2 sts, blo dc in next 6 sts] around, join to first dc made, fasten off. *<192 blo dc, 32 dc, 16 ch-8 sp>*

BALANCE
MANDALA

COMFORT
MANDALA

verb. to soothe, console, or reassure; bring cheer to
crochet and comfort; you can't have one without the other, unless you're using black yarn

FINISHED SIZE
42cm/16.5in unblocked

MATERIALS
Naturals Bamboo & Cotton
One ball of each

Colour 1 7131 Peach
Colour 2 7133 Blush
Colour 3 7138 Heather
Colour 4 7139 Wedgewood
Colour 5 7141 Aqua
Colour 6 7127 Chalk

US E-4 / UK 9 / (3.5mm) hook
Yarn Needle
Scissors
Stitch Marker

NOTES & TIPS
Magic Ring
Pull Magic Ring after Round 2 nice and tight, but not too tight, enough to keep all the stitches nice and uniform.

Cure sometimes, treat often, comfort always.

Hippocrates

Round 1: C1 - *Leave a longer tail than normal so you can pull the ring tighter after Rnd 3.*

Make a MR, or (ch 10, join to first ch to form ring), ch 3 *(counts as tr)*, 23 tr in ring, join to top of ch 3, fasten off. *<24 tr>*

Round 2: C2

In any st, make a standing cross over dtr, cross over dtr around, join to first dtr made, do not fasten off. *<12 cross over dtr>*

Round 3: C2

Ch 1 *(doesn't count as st)*, dc in same st as join, 2 dc in ch-1 sp, [dc in next 2 sts, 2 dc in ch-sp] around, on final repeat dc in last st, join to first dc made, fasten off. *<48 dc>*

Round 4: C3

In first dc made, make a standing [puff 3, ch 2, sk st] around, join to first puff 3 made, fasten off. *<24 puff 3, 24 ch-2 sp>*

Round 5: C4

Around any puff, make a standing [fphtr around puff, fold ch-2 sts back, 2 dtr in unworked st from Rnd 4] around, join to first fphtr made, fasten off. *<48 dtr, 24 fphtr>*

Round 6: C5

Around any fphtr, make a standing [fpdc around fphtr, ch 1, (tr, ch 1, tr) in unworked ch-2 sp from Rnd 4, ch 1] around, join to first fpdc, fasten off. *<24 fpdc, 72 ch-1 sp, 48 tr>*

Round 7: C6 – *This rnd is worked only in ch-1 sps between two tr sts from Rnd 6.*

Make a standing [3 tr in ch-1 sp between two tr sts, ch 1] around, join to first tr made, fasten off. *<72 tr>*

Round 8: C1

In any ch-1 sp, make a standing [tr in ch-1 sp, tr in next 3 sts] around, join to first tr made, fasten off. *<96 tr>*

Round 9: C2 – *This rnd may cup up slightly.*

In first tr made in prev rnd, make a standing [dtr in tr made in ch-sp, x st over next 3 sts] around, join to first dtr made, fasten off. *<24 dtr, 24 dtr x st>*

Round 10: C3

In any dtr, make a standing [pop in dtr st, ch 2, dc in next st, ch 2, sk ch-2 sp, dc in next st, ch 2] around, join to first pop made, fasten off. *<24 pop, 72 ch-2 sp, 48 dc>*

Round 11: C4 – *This rnd may be slightly ruffled*

In any pop, make a standing [(tr, ch 2, tr) in pop, tr in ch-2 sp, sk st, (htr, dc, htr) in ch-2 sp, sk st, tr in ch-2 sp] around, join to first tr made, fasten off. *<24 dc, 48 htr, 96 tr, 24 ch-2 sp>*

Round 12: C5 – *This rnd may still be slightly ruffled*

In any ch-2 sp, make a standing [(dc, ch 2, dc) in ch-2 sp, dc in 3rd loop of next 2 sts, ch 2, sk htr, dc in ch-2 sp from Rnd 9, ch 2, sk dc and htr, dc in 3rd loop of next 2 sts] around, join to first dc made, fasten off. *<72 dc, 96*

3rd loop dc, 72 ch-2 sp>

Round 13: C6

In any ch-2 point, make a standing [(dtr2cl, ch 6, dtr2cl) in ch-2 point] around, join to first dtr2cl made, do not fasten off.

<48 dtr2cl, 24 ch-6 sp>

Round 14: C6

Ch 1 (doesn't count as st), dc in same st as join, 6 dc in ch-6 sp, [dc in next 2 sts, 6 dc in ch-6 sp] around, on final repeat dc in last st, fasten off. *<192 dc>*

Round 15: C1 – *Fptr st made around last cl in ch-2 point, and next cl in next ch-2 point together.*

Around first and last cl made, make a standing [fptr around both clusters together, ch 1, sk 2 sts, (tr, ch 1) in each of next 4 sts, sk 2 sts] around, join to first fptr made, fasten off. *<24 fptr, 96 tr, 120 ch-1 sp>*

Round 16: C2

Around any fptr, make a standing [fpdc around fptr, htr in ch-1 sp, {tr in next st, tr in next ch-sp} three times, tr in next st, htr in ch-1 sp] around, join to first fpdc made, fasten off. *<24 fpdc, 48 htr, 168 tr>*

Round 17: C3

In 3rd st after fpdc, make a standing [dc in st, ch 5, sk 3 sts, dc in next st, ch 5, sk 5 sts] around, on final repeat ch 2, tr in first dc made, do not fasten off. *<48 dc, 48 ch-5 sp>*

Round 18: C3

Dc over tr just made *(this will bring you to middle of last ch-5 sp from prev rnd)*, ch 5, [dc in ch-5 sp, ch 5] around, join to first dc made, fasten off. *<48 dc, 48 ch-5 sp>*

Round 19: C4

In any ch-5 sp, make a standing [(3 tr, ch 3) in each ch-5 sp] around, join to first tr made, fasten off. *<144 tr, 48 ch-3 sp>*

Round 20: C5

In any ch-3 sp, make a standing [(2 tr, ch 2, 2 tr) in ch-3 sp, sk st, dc in middle st, sk st] around, join to first tr made, fasten off. *<192 tr, 48 ch-2 sp, 48 dc>*

Round 21: C6

In any ch-2 point, make a standing [(dtr2cl, ch 5, dtr2cl) in ch-2 point] around, join to first dtr2cl made, do not fasten off.

<96 dtr2cl, 48 ch-5 sp>

Round 22: C6

Around first and last cl made, make a standing [fpdc around both clusters together from prev rnd, (3 dc, picot 3, 3 dc) in ch-5 sp] around, join to first fpdc made, fasten off.

<48 picot 3, 288 dc, 48 fpdc>

COMFORT
MANDALA

DEDICATION
MANDALA

noun. the state of being dedicated

Something you see when a crocheter is counting the same round or row of stitches for the 20th time, shhh!

FINISHED SIZE

21cm/8.2in unblocked

MATERIALS

Naturals Organic Cotton
One ball of each

Colour 1 7198 Azure
Colour 2 7195 Faded Denim
Colour 3 7183 Blossom
Colour 4 7169 Fondant

US G-6 / UK 8 / (4mm) hook
Yarn Needle
Scissors
Stitch Marker

NOTES & TIPS

Cluster Stitches

Is your top loop too big and loose? Try holding all the yarn over loops on your hook with a finger before inserting your hook into the stitch. As you make the yarn over and pull through loop, push remaining loops towards the end of the hook, still securing the remaining loops on the hook with your finger.

Dedication, absolute dedication, is what keeps one ahead.

Bruce Lee

Round 1: C1

Make a MR, or (ch 12, join to first ch to form ring), ch 1 (doesn't count as st), 16 dc in ring, join to first dc made, do not fasten off. *<16 dc>*

Round 2: C1

Beg dtr2cl in same st as join, ch 2, (dtr2cl in next st, ch 2) around, join to beg dtr2cl, do not fasten off. *<16 dtr2cl, 16 ch-2 sp>*

Round 3: C1

Ch 1 (doesn't count as st), 3 dc in each ch-2 sp around, join to first dc made, fasten off. *<48 dc>*

Round 4: C2

Around any cl from Rnd 2, make a standing [fptrtr around cl from Rnd 2, ch 1, sk st, puff 3 in next st from Rnd 3, ch 1, sk st] around, join to first fptrtr made, do not fasten off. *<16 fptrtr, 16 puff 3, 32 ch-1 sp>*

Round 5: C2

In any ch-1 sp, make a standing 2 dc in each ch-1 sp around, join to first dc made, fasten off. *<64 dc>*

Round 6: C3

Around any fptrtr from Rnd 4, make a standing [fpdtr around fptrtr from Rnd 4, tr in next 4 sts] around, join to first fpdtr made, do not fasten off. *<16 fpdtr, 64 tr>*

Round 7: C3

Ch 1 (doesn't count as st), dc in each st around, join to first dc made, fasten off. *<80 dc>*

Round 8: C4

In first dc made in prev rnd, make a standing [dtr2cl in st, ch 3, sk st, dc in next 2 sts, ch 3, sk st] around, join to first dtr2cl made, do not fasten off. *<16 dtr2cl, 32 ch-3 sp, 32 dc>*

Round 9: C4

(Beg dtr2cl, ch 7, dtr2cl) in same st as join, (dtr2cl, ch 7, dtr2cl) in each cl around, join to first cl made, do not fasten off. *<32 dtr2cl, 16 ch-7 sp>*

Round 10: C4

Ch 1 (doesn't count as st), dc in same st as join, 7 dc in ch-7 sp, sk st, [dc in next st, 7 dc in ch-7 sp, sk st] around, join to first dc made, fasten off. *<128 dc>*

43

EXCITEMENT
MANDALA

noun. an excited state or condition

There is no excitement quite like that of a crocheter buying more yarn

FINISHED SIZE
21cm/8.2in unblocked

MATERIALS

Naturals Organic Cotton
One ball of each

Colour 1 7175 Citron
Colour 2 7173 Bone
Colour 3 7187 Flax
Colour 4 7182 Pink Clay
Colour 5 7189 Rosewood

US G-6 / UK 8 / (4mm) hook
Yarn Needle
Scissors
Stitch Marker

NOTES & TIPS

Round 6

Sometimes, you can start your standing stitches without a knot already on your hook, this gives the piece an even more uniform, invisible join. But in the instance where you use the same colour in the following round, I recommend using a knot for standing stitches.

I am excited for all of the good things to come.

affirmation

Round 1: C1

Make a MR, or (ch 4, join to first ch to form ring), ch 3 (counts as tr), 11 tr in ring, join to top of ch-3, do not fasten off. *<12 tr>*

Round 2: C1

Beg dtr2cl, ch 2 in same st as join, (dtr2cl, ch 2) in each st around, join to first cl made, fasten off. *<12 dtr2cl, 12 ch-2 sp>*

Round 3: C2

In any ch-2 sp, make a standing 5 tr in each ch-2 sp around, join to first tr made, fasten off. *<60 tr>*

Round 4: C3

Around any cl from rnd 2, make a standing [fptr around cl from rnd 2, sk next st, blo dc in next st, ch 4, sk st, blo dc in next st, sk st] around, join to first fptr made, do not fasten off. *<12 fptr, 24 bloc dc, 12 ch-4 sp>*

Round 5: C3

In any ch-4 sp, make a standing (4 tr, ch 2, 4 tr) in ch-4 sp, sk st, sl st in fptr, sk st] around, fasten off. *<96 tr, 12 sl st, 12 ch-2 sp>*

Round 6: C4

In any ch-2 sp, make a standing [(tr, ch 4, tr) in ch-2 sp, ch 3, sk 9 sts] around, join to first tr made, do not fasten off. *<24 tr, 12 ch-4 sp, 12 ch-3 sp>*

Round 7: C4

Sl st to ch-4 sp, (beg tr2cl, ch 1, tr2cl, ch 3, tr2cl, ch 1, tr2cl) in same sp, ch 2, sk st, dc in ch-3 sp, ch 2, [(tr2cl, ch 1, tr2cl, ch 3, tr2cl, ch 1, tr2cl) in ch-4 sp, ch 2, sk st, dc in ch-3 sp, ch 2, sk st] around, join to first cl made, fasten off. *<12 dc, 24 ch-2 sp, 12 ch-3 sp, 24 ch-1 sp, 48 tr2cl>*

Round 8: C5

In any ch-3 sp, make a standing [(2 htr, ch-2, 2 htr) in ch-3 sp, fphtr around cl, htr in ch-1 sp, fphtr around cl, 2 htr in ch-2 sp, sl st in dc, 2 htr in ch-2 sp, fphtr around cl, htr in ch-1 sp, fphtr around cl] around, join to first htr made, fasten off. *<12 sl st, 120 htr, 48 fphtr>*

EXPLORATION
MANDALA

noun. an act or instance of exploring or investigating; examination

Crocheters do this when they're looking for yarn they know they have 'somewhere' in their stash....

FINISHED SIZE
14.5cm/5.7in unblocked

MATERIALS
Naturals Organic Cotton
One ball of each

Colour 1 7168 Gypsum
Colour 2 7178 Papaya
Colour 3 7180 Coral
Colour 4 7174 Buttermilk
Colour 5 7201 Indigo Wash
Colour 6 7199 Deep Sea
Colour 7 7172 Peppermint

US G-6 / UK 8 / (4mm) hook
Yarn Needle
Scissors

NOTES & TIPS

Third Loop
Work in the loop behind the 'V' as stated.

Magic Ring
After Round 2, pull Magic Ring nice and tight, but not too tight, enough to keep all the stitches nice and uniform.

Exploration is curiosity put into action

Don Walsh

Round 1: C1

Make a MR, or (ch 4, join to first ch to form ring), ch 1 (doesn't count as st), 8 dc in ring, join to first dc, do not fasten off. *<8 dc>*

Round 2: C1

Beg dtr4cl in same st as join, ch 3, (dtr4cl, ch 3) in each st around, join to first cl made, fasten off. *<8 dtr4cl, 8 ch-3 sp>*

Round 3: C2

Around any cl, make a standing [fphtr around cl, 4 htr in ch-3 sp] around, join to first htr made, fasten off. *<8 fphtr, 32 htr>*

Round 4: C3

Around any fphtr, make a standing [(fptr, ch 1, fptr) around fphtr, blo htr in next 4 sts] around, join to first fptr made, fasten off. *<16 fptr, 8 ch-1 sp, 32 blo htr>*

Round 5: C4

In any ch-1 sp, make a standing [pop in ch-1 sp, ch-2, sk fptr, blo dc in next 2 sts, ch 1, blo dc in next 2 sts, ch 2, sk fptr] around, join to first pop made, fasten off. *<8 pop, 8 ch-1 sp, 32 blo dc, 16 ch-2 sp>*

Round 6: C1

In any pop, make a standing [dc in pop, ch 1, sk (ch-2 sp, 2 dc), (4 dtr, picot 3, 4 dtr) in ch-1 sp, ch 1, sk (2 dc, ch-2 sp)] around, join to first dc made, fasten off. *<64 dtr, 8 picot 3, 8 dc, 16 ch-1 sp>*

51

FEARLESS
MANDALA

adjective. without fear; bold or brave; intrepid
A crocheter is fearless, especially when it comes to frogging.

FINISHED SIZE
30cm/11.8in unblocked

MATERIALS
Naturals Bamboo & Cotton
One ball of each

Colour 1 7128 Ecru
Colour 2 7147 Nutmeg
Colour 3 7161 Umber
Colour 4 7144 Surf
Colour 5 7152 Indigo

US E/4; UK 9; (3.5mm) hook
Yarn Needle
Scissors

NOTES & TIPS

Clusters
Pay attention to your placement of the cluster stitches in Round 4. Note that half is done on either side of the popcorn stitch.

Magic Ring
After Round 2, pull Magic Ring nice and tight, but not too tight, enough to keep all the stitches nice and uniform.

Once you become fearless, life becomes limitless.

Nishant Patel & Mit Bhatt

Round 1: C1

Make a MR, or (ch 4, join to first ch to form ring), ch 3 (counts as tr), 11 tr in ring, join with sl st to top of ch-3, do not fasten off. *<12 tr>*

Round 2: C1

Ch 4 (counts as tr + ch 1), (tr, ch 1) in each st around, join with sl st to 3rd ch, do not fasten off. *<12 tr, 12 ch-1 sp>*

Round 3: C1

Beg pop in same st as join, ch 3, sk ch-sp, [pop in st, ch 3, sk ch-sp] around, join to first pop made, fasten off. *<12 pop, 12 ch-3 sp>*

Round 4: C2

In any ch-3 sp before pop, make a standing [dtr6cl (3 legs on one side of the pop and 3 legs on the other), ch 8] around, join to first dtr6cl made, fasten off.

<12 dtr6cl, 12 ch-8 sp>

Round 5: C3

In any cl, make a standing [fpdc around cl, (5 dc, ch 2, 5 dc) in ch-8 sp] around, join to first fpdc made, fasten off. *<12 fpdc, 120 dc, 12 ch-2 sp>*

Round 6: C4

Make a standing [(dc, ch 2, dc) in ch-2 sp, ch 10] around, join to first dc made, do not fasten off. *<24 dc, 12 ch-10 sp, 12 ch-2 sp>*

Round 7: C4

Ch 1 (doesn't count as st), [(dc, ch 2, dc) in ch-2 sp, sk st, (6 dc, ch 2, 6 dc) in ch-10 sp, sk st] around, join to first dc made, fasten off. *<168 dc, 24 ch-2 sp>*

Round 8: C5

Make a standing [3 dc in higher ch-2 sp, ch 3, (dtr, ch 1, dtr) in lower ch-2 sp, ch 3] around, join to first dc made, do not fasten off. *<36 dc, 24 dtr, 12 ch-1 sp, 24 ch-3 sp, 12 ch-1 sp>*

Round 9: C5

Ch 3 (counts a tr), tr in next 2 sts, 3 tr in ch-3 sp, tr in next st, tr in ch-sp, tr in next st, 3 tr in ch-3 sp, [tr in next 3 sts, 3 tr in ch-3 sp, tr in next st, tr in ch-sp, tr in next st, 3 tr in ch-3 sp] around, join to top of ch-3, fasten off. *<144 tr>*

Round 10: C1

Make a fptr around first tr made in prev rnd, fptr around each st around, join to first fptr made, fasten off. *<144 fptr>*

Round 11: C2

In first fptr made, make a standing tr, tr in next 2 sts, ch 3, sk 3 sts, [tr in next 3 sts, ch 3, sk 3 sts] around, join to first tr made, fasten off. *<72 tr, 24 ch-3 sp>*

Round 12: C3

In first tr made in prev rnd, make a standing tr in st, tr in next 2 sts, (tr, ch 2, tr) in ch-3 sp, [tr in next 3 sts, (tr, ch 2, tr) in ch-3 sp] around, join to first tr made, fasten off. *<120 tr, 24 ch-2 sp>*

Round 13: C4

In any middle tr, make a standing [pop in

middle tr from Rnd 12, ch 5, dc into ch-3 sp from Rnd 11, ch 5] around, join to first pop made, fasten off. *<24 pop, 24 dc, 48 ch-5 sp>*

Round 14: C5

Around any dc, make a standing [fpdc around dc, (2 htr, 3 tr) in ch-5 sp, (tr, ch 2, tr) in pop, (3 tr, 2 htr) in ch-5 sp] around, join to first fpdc made, fasten off. *<96 htr, 24 fpdc,*

FEARLESS
MANDALA

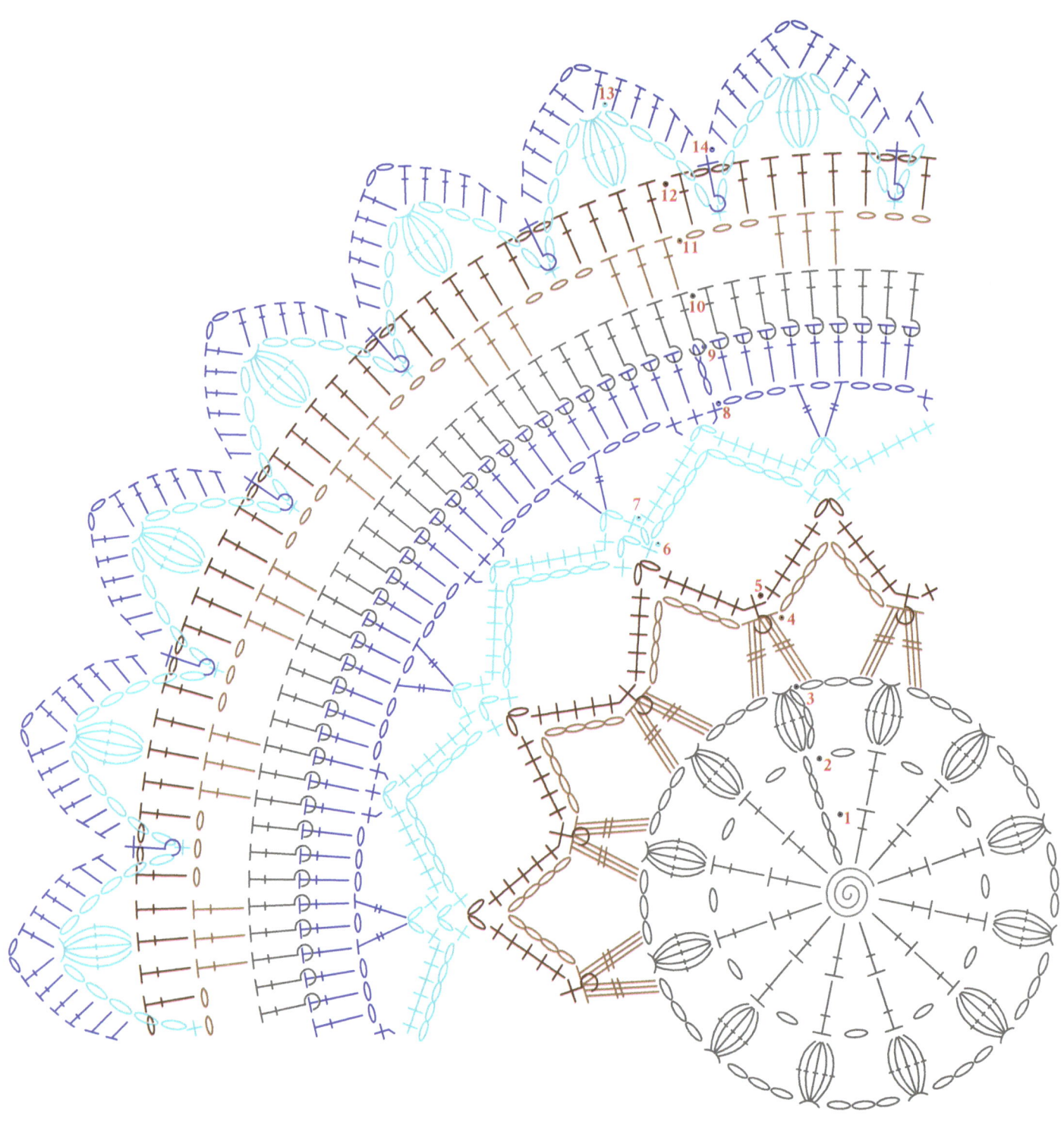

56

FOCUS
MANDALA

noun. close attention or concentration
Crocheters need to do this in order to avoid frogging.

FINISHED SIZE
11cm/4.3in unblocked

MATERIALS
Naturals Bamboo & Cotton
One ball

Colour 1 7126 Spring Green

US E/4; UK 9; (3.5mm) hook
Yarn Needle
Scissors

NOTES & TIPS

Blocking
Depending on what yarn you use, this little motif may need a block to showcase its picots.

Magic Ring
After Round 2, pull Magic Ring nice and tight, but not too tight, enough to keep all the stitches nice and uniform

Where focus goes, energy flows. And where energy flows, whatever you're focusing on grows.
Tony Robbins

Round 1:
Make a MR, or (ch 3, join to first ch to form ring), ch 1 (doesn't count as st here and throughout), 6 dc in ring, join to first dc made. *<6 dc>*

Round 2:
Ch 6 (counts as tr + ch 3), (tr, ch 3) in each st around, join to top of 3rd ch.
<6 tr, 6 ch-3 sp>

Round 3:
Ch 1, dc in same st as join, 3 dc in ch-3 sp, [dc in st, 3 dc in ch-3 sp] around, join to first dc made. *<24 dc>*

Round 4:
Ch 4, sl st in same st as join, dc in next 3 sts, [(sl st, ch 4, sl st) in next st, dc in next 3 sts] around, join in same st as Rnd 3 join.
<18 dc, 12 sl st, 6 ch-4 sp>

Round 5:
Sl st to ch-4 sp, (beg dtr3cl, ch 3, dtr3cl) in same sp, ch 4, sk dc, dc in next st, ch 4, sk next st, [(dtr3cl, ch 3, dtr3cl) in ch-4 sp, ch 4, sk next dc, dc in next st, ch 4, sk next dc st] around, join to top of beg dtr3cl
<12 dtr3cl, 6 dc, 6 ch-3 sp, 12 ch-4 sp>

Round 6:
Ch 1, [(dc, picot 3) in same st as join, (2 dc, picot 5, 2 dc) in ch-3 sp, (dc, picot 3) in next st, 4 dc in each of next 2 ch-4 sps] around, join to first dc made, fasten off.
<84 dc, 12 picot 3, 6 picot 5>

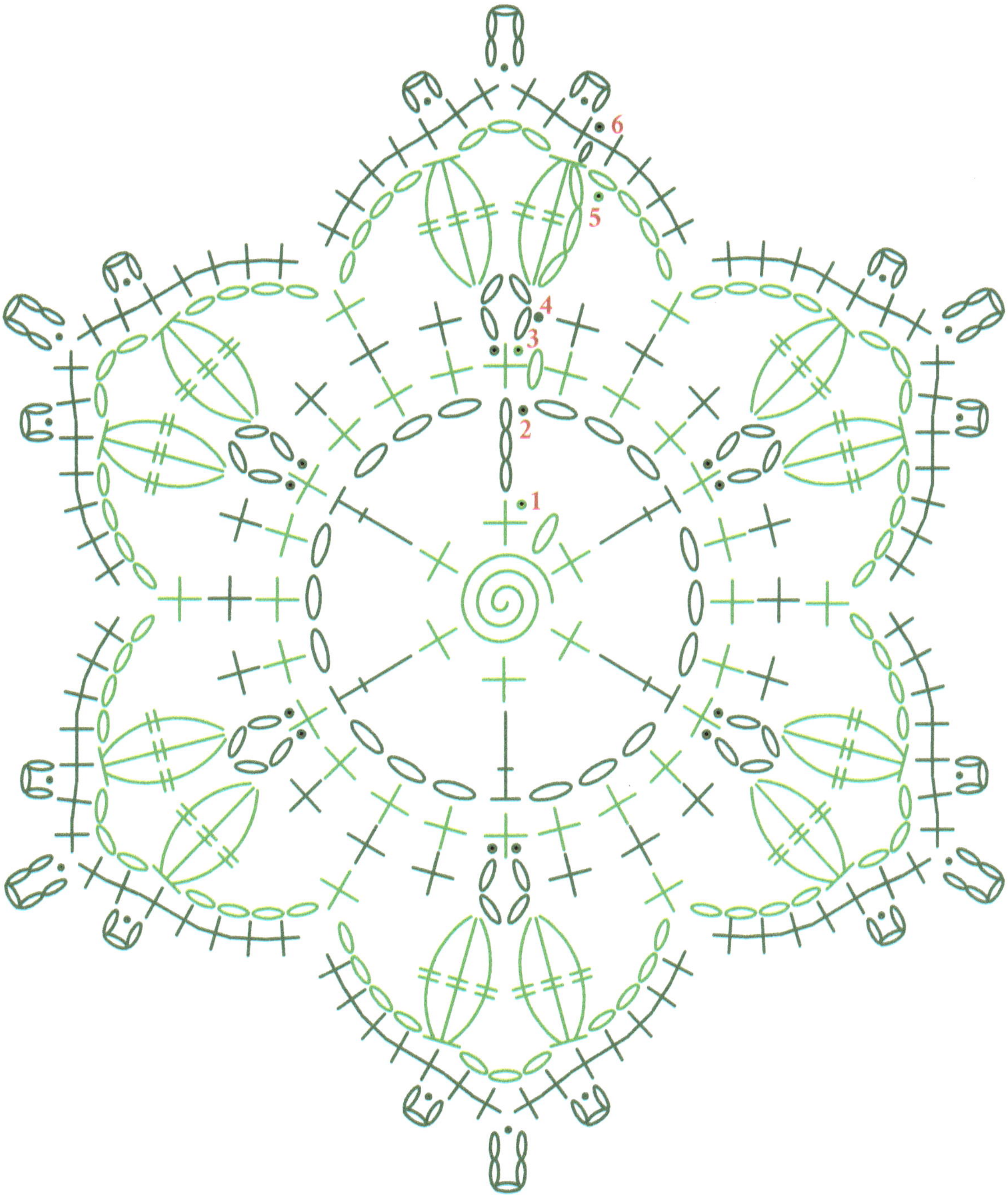

61

GOODNESS
MANDALA

noun. the state or quality of being good; moral excellence; virtue

The goodness that comes along with crocheting is the friendships that form for life.

FINISHED SIZE

6.5cm/2.5in unblocked

MATERIALS

Naturals Bamboo & Cotton
One ball of each

Colour 1 7128 Ecru
Colour 2 7162 Powder Blue
Colour 3 7165 Rose
Colour 4 7154 Pumice

US E-4 / UK 9 / (3.5mm) hook
Yarn Needle
Scissors

NOTES & TIPS

Colour Placement

Have fun playing around with colour in this pattern. The pattern has the guides for colour changes, so just make note when to start and finish each one.

Round 3

Fold round 2 slightly forward, you will see 2 prominent loops that stick out. This is where you will make your slip stitch. If you find it too difficult, you could slip stitch into the 3rd loop instead.

Goodness is about character - integrity, honesty, kindness, generosity, moral courage, and the like. More than anything else, it is about how we treat other people.

Dennis Prager

Round 1: C1

Make a MR, or (ch 4, join to first ch to form ring), ch 3 (counts as tr), 11 tr in ring, join to top of ch-3, fasten off. *<12 tr>*

Round 2: C2

In any st, make a standing (tr, dc) in each st around, join to first tr made, fasten off. *<12 tr, 12 dc>*

Round 3: C3 – Fold Rnd 2 slightly forward, the loops of tr post are on the back of the st

In any tr, [sl st into both loops of tr post from Rnd 2, ch 2] around, sl st to same st as first sl st made, do not fasten off. *<12 sl st, 12 ch-2 sp>*

Round 4: C3

3 dc in each ch-2 sp around, skipping sl st, join to first dc made, fasten off. *<36 dc>*

Round 5: C4

Around any sl st, make a standing [fpdc around sl st from Rnd 3, sk st, 5 tr in next st on Rnd 4, sk st] around, join to first fpdc made, fasten off. *<12 fpdc, 60 tr>*

RND 3 - PHOTOS OF LOOPS TO WORK INTO WRONG SIDE SHOWING (BACK)

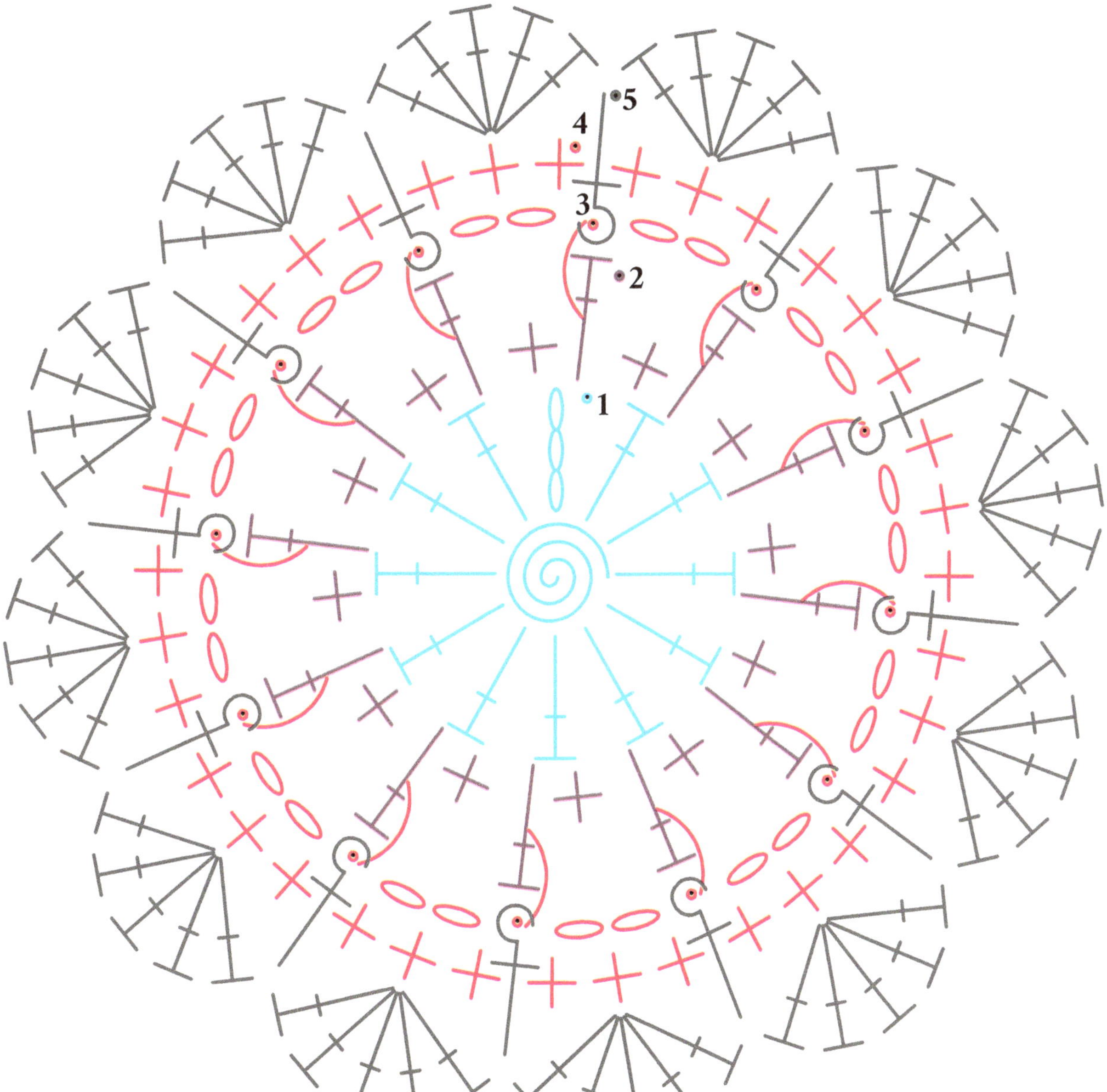

65

GRATITUDE
MANDALA

noun. the quality or feeling of being grateful or thankful

What crocheters feel when they see the postman after probably stalking them for too long.

FINISHED SIZE
14.5cm/5.7in unblocked

MATERIALS
Naturals Organic Cotton
One ball of each

Colour 1 7181 Carrot
Colour 2 7179 Flamingo
Colour 3 7185 Amethyst
Colour 4 7198 Azure
Colour 5 7191 Jade
Colour 6 7171 Leaf

US G-6 / UK 8 / (4mm) hook
Yarn Needle
Scissors

NOTES & TIPS
Stitch Count
Triple check the Round 1 stitch count - don't do what I did and just thought 'Oh yeah, that looks about it'...turns out I had completely missed like 12 stitches so my piece didn't lie flat.

Helps you see what is there instead of what is not.

Round 1: C1

Make a MR, or (ch 14, join to first ch to form ring), ch 3 (counts as tr here and throughout), 27 tr in ring, join to top of ch-3, do not fasten off. *<28 tr>*

Round 2: C1

Ch 5 (counts as dtr + ch 1), (dtr, ch 1) in each st around, join to fourth ch, fasten off.

<28 dtr, 28 ch-1 sp>

Round 3: C2

In any dtr st, make a standing [htr in st, htr in ch-1 sp] around, join to first htr made, do not fasten off. *<56 htr>*

Round 4: C2

Ch 10 (counts as tr + ch 7), sk 3 sts, [tr in next st, ch 7, sk 3 sts] around, join to ch-3, fasten off. *<14 tr, 14 ch-7 sp>*

Round 5: C3

In any ch-7 sp, make a standing [2 tr in ch-7 sp, ch 6, sk st] around, join to first tr made, do not fasten off. *<28 tr, 14 ch-6 sp>*

Round 6: C3

Sl st to ch-6 sp, ch 3, (3 tr, ch 2, 4 tr) in same sp, sk 2 sts, [(4 tr, ch 2, 4 tr) in ch-6 sp, sk 2 sts] around, join to top of third ch, fasten off. *<112 tr, 14 ch-2 sp>*

Round 7: C4

In any ch-2 sp, make a standing [2 tr in ch-2 sp, ch 12, sk 8 sts] around, join to first tr made, do not fasten off. *<28 tr, 14 ch-12 sp>*

Round 8: C4

Sl st in next st and next 2 ch-sts, sl st in ch-12 sp, beg tr2cl, ch 2, [(tr2cl, ch 2) 4 times, tr2cl] in same sp, sk 2 sts, *([tr2cl, ch 2] 5 times, tr2cl) in ch-12 sp, sk 2 sts; rep from * around, join to first cl made, fasten off.

<84 tr2cl, 70 ch-2 sp>

Round 9: C5

In any middle ch-2 sp, make a standing [(tr, ch 3, tr) in middle ch-2 sp, ch 6, sk next (st, ch-2 sp, st), sl st in next ch-2 sp, ch 4, sk 2 sts, sl st in next ch-2 sp, ch 6, sk next (st, ch-2 sp, st)] around, join to first tr made, do not fasten off. *<28 sl st, 28 tr, 14 ch-3 sp, 28 ch-6 sp, 14 ch-4 sp>*

Round 10: C5

Ch 3, (2 tr, ch 3, 2 tr) in ch-3 sp, tr in next st, 5 tr in ch-6 sp, sk sl st, sl st in ch-4 sp, sk sl st, 5 tr in ch-6 sp, [tr in next st, (2 tr, ch 3, 2 tr) in ch-3 sp, tr in next st, 5 tr in ch-6 sp, sk sl st, sl st in ch-4 sp, sk sl st, 5 tr in ch-6 sp] around, join to top of ch-3, fasten off. *<224 tr, 14 ch-3 sp, 14 sl st>*

69

HAPPINESS
MANDALA

noun. an excited state or condition.

What crocheters feel when they finish their current wip and weave in the very last end.

FINISHED SIZE

10cm/3.9in unblocked

MATERIALS

Naturals Bamboo & Cotton
One ball of each

Colour 1 7128 Ecru
Colour 2 7130 Apricot
Colour 3 7131 Peach
Colour 4 7132 Pale Pink
Colour 5 7133 Blush

US E-4 / UK 9 / (3.5mm) hook
Yarn Needle
Scissors

NOTES & TIPS

Round 5
Pay attention to where the htr stitches are placed. Don't make a boo-boo and forget to skip the dc stitches.

Happiness depends upon ourselves

Aristotle

Round 1: C1

Make a MR, or (ch 4, join to first ch to form ring), ch 3 (counts as tr), 11 tr in ring, join to top of ch-3, do not fasten off. *<12 tr>*

Round 2: C1

Sl st to next st, beg dtr3cl, ch 2, dtr in next st, ch 2, [dtr3cl in next st, ch 2, dtr in next st, ch 2] around, join to first cl made, fasten off.

<6 dtr3cl, 6 dtr, 12 ch-2 sp>

Round 3: C2

In any cl, make a standing [dc in cl, 3 dc in ch-2 sp, dc in dtr, 3 dc in ch-2 sp] around, join to first dc made. Fasten off. *<48 dc>*

Round 4: C3

In dc made in cl, make a standing [7 dc in st, sk 2 sts, dc in next st, fptr around dtr from Rnd 2, sk st behind fptr, dc in next st, sk 2 sts] around, join to first tr made. Fasten off. *<6 fptr, 12 dc, 42 tr>*

Round 5: C1 - *Htr sts are worked in third loop only, sk dc from Rnd 4.*

Make a standing [fpdc around fptr, sk st, (htr in next st, 2 htr in next st) three times, htr in next st, sk st] around, join to first fpdc made. Fasten off. *<6 fpdc, 60 htr in 3rd loop>*

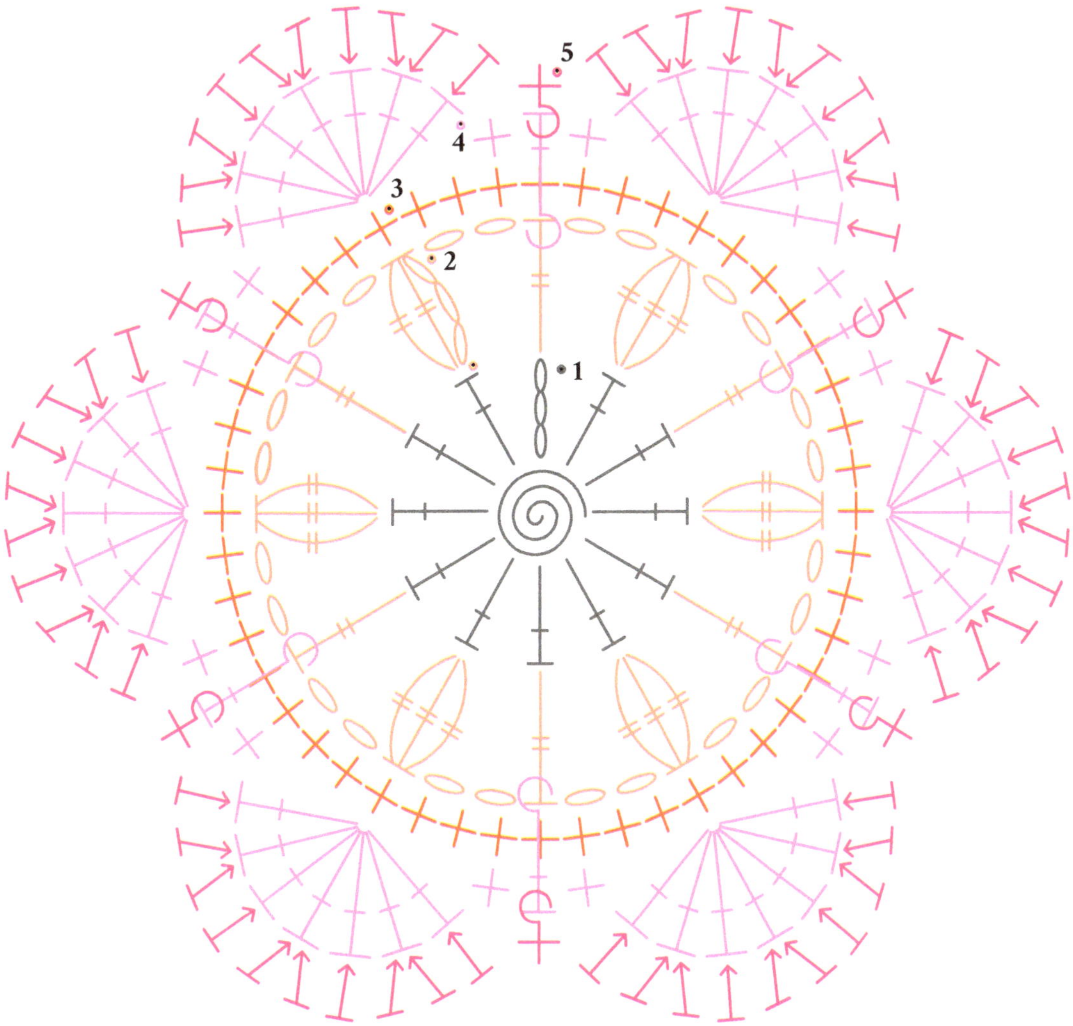

73

HONESTY
MANDALA

noun. truthfulness, sincerity or frankness

What you need in a crochet friend when you are unsure of your colour selection.

FINISHED SIZE

14.5cm/5.7in unblocked

MATERIALS

Naturals Organic Cotton
One ball of each

Colour 1 7187 Flax
Colour 2 7173 Bone
Colour 3 7195 Faded Denim
Colour 4 7200 Blue Dusk

US G-6 / UK 8 / (4mm) hook

Yarn Needle

Scissors

NOTES & TIPS

Attaching to a ring

This mandala would look gorgeous attached to a ring in the picots only. Are you feeling intrigued yet? Are you going to try it?

Never say sorry for being honest

Buddha

Round 1: C1

Make a MR, or (ch 6, join to first ch to form ring), ch 3 (counts as tr here and throughout), 15 tr in ring, join to top of ch-3, fasten off. *<16 tr>*

Round 2: C2

In any st, make a standing [dtr in st, ch 2, dtr3cl in next st, ch 2] around, join to first dtr made, fasten off. *<8 dtr, 8 dtr3cl, 16 ch-2 sp>*

Round 3: C3

In any ch-2 sp, make a standing 3 tr in each ch-2 sp around, join to first tr made, fasten off. *<48 tr>*

Round 4: C4

In any middle tr, make a standing [(tr, ch 3, tr) in middle tr, sk 2 sts] around, join to first tr made, fasten off. *<32 tr, 16 ch-3 sp>*

Round 5: C1

In any ch-3 sp, make a standing [(2 tr, ch 2, 2 tr) in ch-3 sp, sk 2 sts] around, join to first tr made, do not fasten off. *<64 tr, 16 ch-2 sp>*

Round 6: C1

Sl st to ch-2 sp, ch 3 (counts as st), (2 tr, ch 2, 3 tr) in same sp, sk 2 sts, sl st in between the two sets of tr sts, sk 2 sts, [(3 tr, ch 2, 3 tr) in ch-2 sp, sk 2 sts, sl st in between the two sets of tr sts, sk 2 sts] around, join to top of ch 3, fasten off. *<96 tr, 16 ch-2 sp, 16 sl st>*

Round 7: C2

Starting at first tr made in prev rnd, make a standing [bpdc around each of next 3 sts, (dc, ch 2, dc) in ch-2 sp, bpdc around each of next 3 sts, ch 1, sk sl st] around, join to first bpdc made, fasten off.

<96 bpdc, 16 ch-1 sp, 32 dc, 16 ch-2 sp>

Round 8: C3

In any ch-2 sp, make a standing [(dtr2cl, ch 7, dtr2cl) in ch-2 sp, sk 8 sts] around, join to first cl made, fasten off.

<32 dtr2cl, 16 ch-7 sp>

Round 9: C4

In any ch-7 sp, make a standing [(5 htr, picot 3, 5 htr) in ch-7 sp, sl st in between clusters] around, join to first dc made, fasten off. *<160 htr, 16 picot 3, 16 sl st >*

INSPIRE
MANDALA

verb. to fill with an animating, quickening, or exalting influence
Never interrupt a crocheter trying to find inspiration on Pinterest.

FINISHED SIZE
42cm/16.5in unblocked

MATERIALS

Special Aran
One ball of each

Colour 1 1320 Denim
Colour 2 1722 Storm Blue
Colour 3 1725 Sage
Colour 4 1712 Lime
Colour 5 1823 Mustard

US H-8 / UK 6 / (5mm) hook
Yarn Needle
Scissors
3mm Beads (see below)

NOTES & TIPS

Beads required
Round 3: 12 Beads
Round 8: 24 Beads
Round 10: 24 Beads
Feel free to complement (match) or contrast (opposite) the colours in your rounds with the beads.

there is inspiration all around us.

Kapil Dev

Round 1: C1

Make a MR, or (ch 8, join to first ch to form ring), ch 1 (doesn't count as st here and throughout), 12 dc in ring, join to first dc made, do not fasten off. *<12 dc>*

Round 2: C1

Beg dtr2cl, ch 2, (dtr2cl, ch 2) in each st around, join to first cl made, do not fasten off. *<12 dtr2cl, 12 ch-2 sp>*

Round 3: C1

Ch 1, [dc in st, (dc, ch 1, IB, ch 1, dc) in ch-2 sp] around, join to first dc made, fasten off. *<36 dc, 12 beads, 24 ch-1 sp>*

Round 4: C2 – This round is worked in the middle dc between beads from Rnd 3 only

In middle dc between beads, make a standing [(dtr, ch 3, dtr) in middle dc, ch 1, sk st, sk bead, sk st] around, join to first dtr made, do not fasten off. *<24 dtr, 12 ch-3 sp, 12 ch-1 sp>*

Round 5: C2

Ch 3 (counts as tr), 3 tr in ch-3 sp, tr in next st, tr in ch-1 sp, place marker in this tr only, [tr in next st, 3 tr in ch-3 sp, tr in next st, tr in ch-1 sp] around, join to top of ch-3, fasten off. *<72 tr>*

Round 6: C3

In marked st, make a standing tr, tr in each st around, join to first tr made, do not fasten off. *<72 tr>*

Round 7: C3

Beg dtr2cl, (ch 4, dtr2cl) in same st, sk 2 sts, [(dtr2cl, ch 4, dtr2cl) in next st, sk 2 sts] around, join to first cl made, fasten off. *<48 dtr2cl, 24 ch-4 sp>*

Round 8: C4

In any ch-4 sp, make a standing [(2 htr, tr, ch 1, IB, ch 1, tr, 2 htr) in ch-4 sp, fphtr2tog around next 2 cl] around, join to first htr made, fasten off. *<96 htr, 48 tr, 48 ch-1 sp, 24 beads, 24 fphtr2tog>*

Round 9: C5

In any loop behind any bead, make a standing [(dtr2cl, ch 6, dtr2cl) in each loop behind the bead] around, join to first cl made, do not fasten off. *<48 dtr2cl, 24 ch-6 sp>*

Round 10: C5

In any ch-6 sp, make a standing [(dc, htr, 2 tr, 2 dtr, picot 3, 2 dtr, 2 tr, htr, dc) in ch-6 sp, IB, sk st, sl st in between cl, sk st] around, join to first dc made, fasten off. *<48 dc, 48 htr, 96 tr, 96 dtr, 24 picot 3, 24 beads, 24 sl st>*

81

INTEGRITY
MANDALA

noun. adherence to moral and ethical principles; soundness of moral character; honesty

Integrity is your destiny, it is the light that guides your way - Plato

FINISHED SIZE
19cm/7.5in unblocked

MATERIALS

Naturals Organic Cotton
One ball of each

Colour 1 7183 Blossom
Colour 2 7178 Papaya
Colour 3 7180 Coral
Colour 4 7176 Peach
Colour 5 7174 Buttermilk
Colour 6 7193 Artichoke

US G-6 / UK 8 / (4mm) hook

Yarn Needle

Scissors

NOTES & TIPS

Project Idea

Join these motifs together to make a pretty table runner.
See next page for instructions.

Integrity is doing the right thing, even when no one is watching.

C.S Lewis

Round 1: C1

Make a MR, or (ch 9, join to first ch to form ring), ch 1 (doesn't count as st), 16 dc in ring, join to first dc made, do not fasten off. <16 dc>

Round 2: C1

Beg tr2cl, ch 2, (tr2cl, ch 2) in each st around, join to first cl made, fasten off. <16 tr2cl, 16 ch-2 sp>

Round 3: C2

Around any cl, make a standing [fphtr around cl, 2 htr in ch-2 sp] around, join to first fphtr made, fasten off. <16 fphtr, 32 htr>

Round 4: C3

Make a standing tr in each st around, join to first tr made, fasten off. <48 tr>

Round 5: C4

In tr made in fphtr, make a standing [puff 3, ch 2, sk st] around, join to first puff 3 made, fasten off. <24 puff 3, 24 ch-2 sp>

Round 6: C5

In any ch-2 sp, make a standing [(2 tr, ch 4, 2 tr) in ch-2 sp, ch 1, sk st, sk ch-2 sp, sk st] around, join to first tr made, do not fasten off. <48 tr, 12 ch-4 sp, 12 ch-1 sp>

Round 7: C5

Ch 1 (doesn't count as st), dc in same st as join, sk st, (4 tr, ch 2, 4 tr) in ch-4 sp, sk st, dc in next st, dc in ch-1 sp, [dc in next st, sk st, (4 tr, ch 2, 4 tr) in ch-4 sp, sk st, dc in next st, dc in ch-1 sp] around, join to first dc made, fasten off. <96 tr, 36 dc, 12 ch-2 sp>

Round 8: C6

In any ch-2 sp, make a standing [(dc, ch 2, dc) in ch-2 sp, bphtr around next 4 sts, ch 1, sk st, pop in next, ch 1, sk st, bphtr around next 4 sts] around, join to first dc made, fasten off. <12 pop, 24 dc, 96 bphtr, 12 ch-2 sp>

Joining Motifs:

Make one complete motif.
On consecutive motifs, join in the ch-2 sp on Round 8, but replace the ch-2 with a dc in the complete motif's ch-2 sp of Round 8, then work Round 8 back on the working motif. Join in two points.

85

JOY
MANDALA

noun. the emotion of great delight or happiness caused by something exceptionally good or satisfying; keen pleasure; elation

What crocheters feel when they walk into a yarn store, buy yarn or meet a fellow crocheter.

FINISHED SIZE
14cm/5.5in unblocked

MATERIALS
Naturals Organic Cotton
One ball

Colour 1 7191 Jade

US G-6 / UK 8 / (4mm) hook
Yarn Needle
Scissors

NOTES & TIPS
Project Idea
Need a gift idea?
This motif works up nice and quick and sits lovely and flat, making it the ideal mandala for a coaster to gift.

When the mind is pure, joy follows like a shadow that never leaves.

Buddha

Round 1:
Make a MR, or (ch 6, join to first ch to form ring), ch 1 (doesn't count as st), 12 dc in ring, join to first dc made, do not fasten off. <12 dc>

Round 2:
Ch 4 (counts as tr + ch 1), (tr, ch 1) in each st around, join to third ch of beg ch-4, do not fasten off. <12 tr, 12 ch-1 sp>

Round 3:
Sl st to ch-1 sp, ch 3 (counts as tr here and throughout), 2 tr in same sp, sk st, [3 tr in ch-1 sp, sk st] around, join to top of ch-3, do not fasten off. <36 tr>

Round 4:
Sl st to middle tr, ch 3, 2 tr in same st, ch 1, sk 2 sts, [3 tr in next st, ch 1, sk 2 sts] around, join to top of ch-3, do not fasten off. <36 tr, 12 ch-1 sp>

Round 5:
Beg tr3dec, ch 5, [tr3dec, ch 5, sk ch-1 sp] around, join to first tr3dec made, do not fasten off. <12 tr3dec, 12 ch-5 sp>

Round 6:
[(Dc, htr, 2 tr, ch 2, 2 tr, htr, dc) in ch-5 sp, sl st in tr3dec] around, fasten off. <24 dc, 24 htr, 48 tr, 12 ch-2 sp, 12 sl st>

89

KINDNESS
MANDALA

noun. the state or quality of being kind
Showing kindness; weaving in your friend's ends without being asked.

FINISHED SIZE
21cm/8.2in unblocked

MATERIALS
Naturals Organic Cotton
One ball

Colour 1 7179 Flamingo

US G-6 / UK 8 / (4mm) hook
Small hook to insert beads
(anything from US B1 2.25 - UK 12 2.5mm)
Yarn Needle
Scissors
3mm Beads x 24

NOTES & TIPS
Project Idea
Jar or bowl cover
Have fun playing with colour and maybe coloured beads like I have done here :)

No act of kindness, no matter how small, is ever wasted

Aesop

Round 1:
Make a MR, or (ch 6, join to first ch to form ring), ch 1 (doesn't count as st), 12 dc in ring, join to first dc made, do not fasten off. *<12 dc>*

Round 2:
Ch 4 (counts as tr + ch 1), (tr, ch 1) in each st around, join to third ch of beg ch-4, do not fasten off. *<12 tr, 12 ch-1 sp>*

Round 3:
Sl st to ch-1 sp, ch 3 (counts as tr here and throughout), 2 tr in same sp, sk st, [3 tr in ch-1 sp, sk st] around, join to top of ch-3, do not fasten off. *<36 tr>*

Round 4:
Sl st to middle tr, ch 3, 2 tr in same st, ch 1, sk 2 sts, [3 tr in next st, ch 1, sk 2 sts] around, join to top of ch-3, do not fasten off. *<36 tr, 12 ch-1 sp>*

Round 5:
Sl st to middle tr, ch 3, tr in same st, ch 1, sk st, 2 tr in ch-1 sp, ch 1, sk st, [2 tr in next st, ch 1, sk st, 2 tr in ch-1 sp, ch 1, sk st] around, join to top of ch-3, do not fasten off. *<48 tr, 24 ch-1 sp>*

Round 6:
Sl st to ch-1 sp, beg tr3cl, ch 2, sk 2 sts, [tr3cl in ch-1 sp, ch 2, sk 2 sts] around, join to first cl made, do not fasten off.
<24 tr3cl, 24 ch-2 sp>

Round 7:
Ch 6 (counts as tr + ch 3), tr in same st, sk 2 ch-sp, (tr, ch 3, tr) in each cl around, join to third ch of beg ch-6, do not fasten off. *<48 tr, 24 ch-3 sp>*

Round 8:
Sl st in first ch of ch-3 sp, dc in ch-3 sp, ch 5, [dc in ch-3 sp, ch 5] around, on last repeat, ch 2, tr into first dc made (this replaces the sl st join and places you at the correct starting point for the next round), do not fasten off. *<24 dc, 24 ch-5 sp>*

Round 9:
Dc in last ch-sp (same as tr join), ch 4, IB, ch 4, sk st, [dc in ch-5 sp, ch 4, IB, ch 4] around, join to first dc, fasten off. *<24 dc, 24 IB, 48 ch-4 sp>*

LOYALTY
MANDALA

noun. the state or quality of being loyal; faithfulness to commitments or obligations
Some crocheters find it a little bit hard to stay loyal to one WIP, that's completely okay.

FINISHED SIZE
13cm/5.11in unblocked

MATERIALS
Naturals Bamboo & Cotton
One ball of each

Colour 1 7128 Ecru
Colour 2 7143 Seafoam
Colour 3 7142 Sky
Colour 4 7140 Cornflower

US E/4; UK 9; (3.5mm) hook
Yarn Needle
Scissors
3mm Beads x 16

NOTES & TIPS

Project Idea
This makes the perfect coaster or wine or glass cover.

Loyalty is rare. If you find it, keep it.

Round 1: C1

Make a MR, or (ch 4, join to first ch to form ring), ch 1 (doesn't count as st), 8 dc in ring, join to first dc made. <8 dc>

Round 2: C2

(Sl st, ch 3, tr, ch 3, sl st) in each st around, fasten off. <16 sl st, 16 ch-3 sp, 8 tr>

Round 3: C1

Make a standing [htr in tr, ch 3] around, join to first htr made, do not fasten off.

<8 htr, 8 ch-3 sp>

Round 4: C1

Sl st to ch-3 sp, ch 2 (counts as htr), 5 htr in ch-3 sp, [sk st, 6 htr in ch-3 sp] around, join to top of ch-2, fasten off. <48 htr>

Round 5: C3

Make a standing tr in first htr made in prev rnd, tr in each st around, join to first tr made, fasten off. <48 tr>

Round 6: C4

In first tr made in prev rnd, make a standing [dtr3cl in tr, ch 4, IB, ch 1, sl st in 3rd ch under bead just made, ch 2, sk 2 sts] around, join to first cl made, fasten off. <16 dtr3cl, 16 Beads>

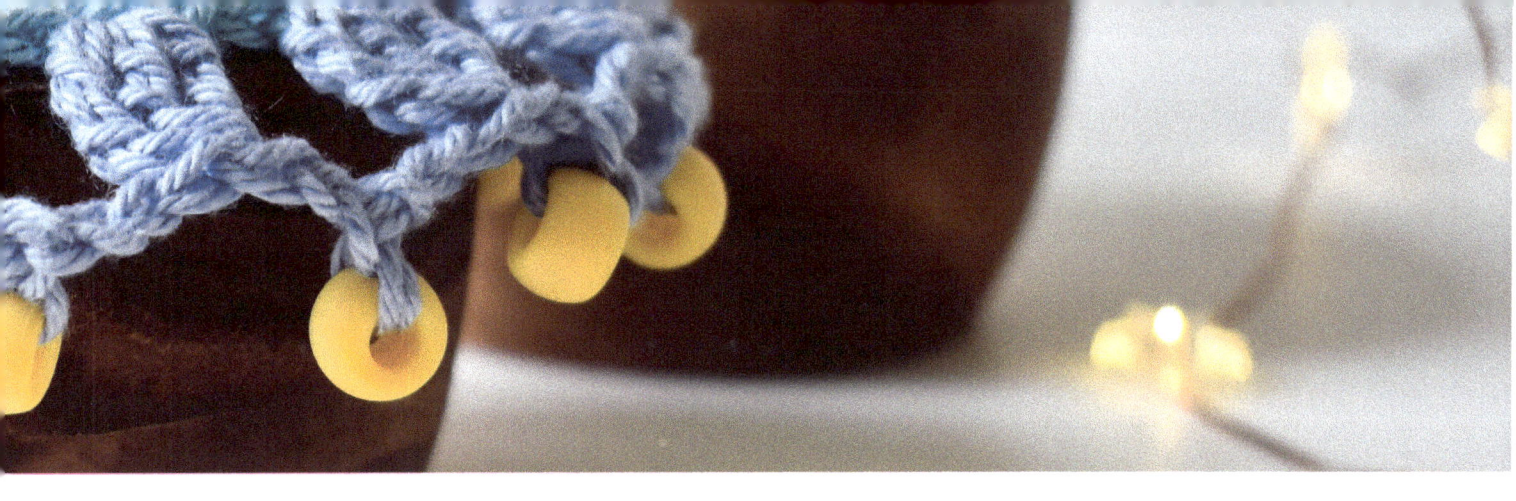

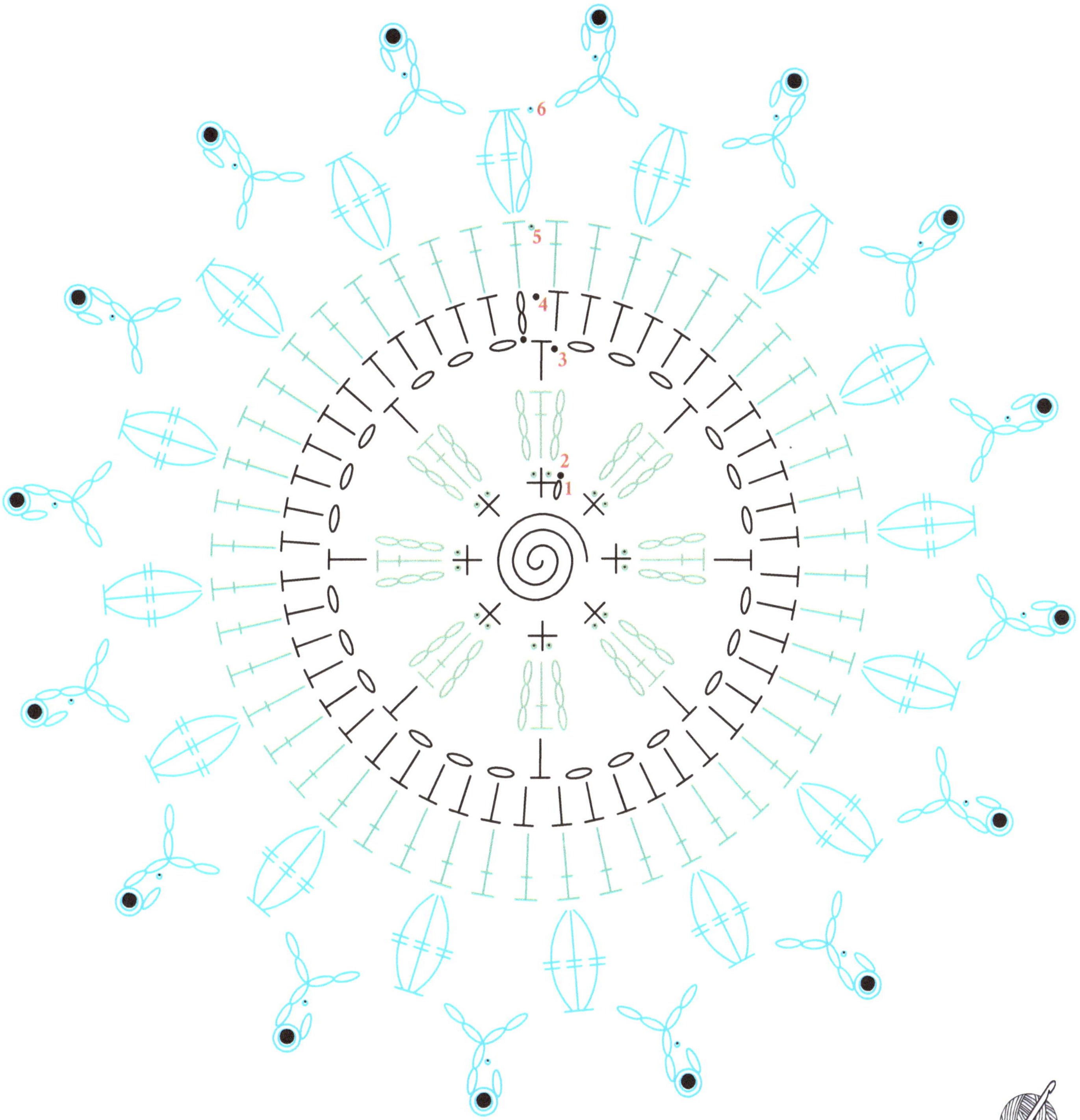

97

MINDFULNESS
MANDALA

noun. the state or quality of being mindful or aware of something
Be present in the moment of each stitch, pay attention to every movement you make.

FINISHED SIZE
30cm/7.5in attached to ring

MATERIALS
Naturals Organic Cotton
One ball of each

Colour 1 7169 Fondant
Colour 2 7177 Blush
Colour 3 7176 Peach
Colour 4 7174 Buttermilk
Colour 5 7172 Peppermint

US G-6 / UK 8 / (4mm) hook
Yarn Needle
Scissors
30cm ring pictured here

NOTES & TIPS
Attach to Ring
Make sure the ring is at least 5-10cm larger than your finished piece as the open-work of this mandala makes it really stretchy.

Mindfulness is being present without judgement in every moment.

Round 1: C1

Make a MR, or (ch 6, join to first ch to form ring), ch 1 (doesn't count as st), 12 dc in ring, join to first dc made, do not fasten off. *<12 dc>*

Round 2: C1

[Ch 3, sl st in next st] around, do not fasten off. *<12 ch-3 sp, 12 sl st>*

Round 3: C1

Sl st to ch-3 sp, beg tr3cl in same sp, ch 4, sk sl st, [tr3cl in ch-3 sp, ch 4, sk sl st] around, join to first cl made, fasten off.

<12 tr3cl, 12 ch-4 sp>

Round 4: C2

Make a standing [(tr3cl, ch 6) in ch-4 sp, sk st] around, join to first cl made, fasten off.

<12 tr3cl, 12 ch-6 sp>

Round 5: C3

Make a standing [(tr3cl, ch 8) in ch-6 sp, sk st] around, join to first cl made, fasten off.

<12 tr3cl, 12 ch-8 sp>

Round 6: C4

Make a standing [(tr3cl, ch 10) in ch-8 sp, sk st] around, join to first cl made, fasten off.

<12 tr3cl, 12 ch-10 sp>

Round 7: C5 - *Optional*

Make a standing [tr3cl in ch-8 sp, ch 7, dc onto ring, ch 7, sk st] around, join to first cl made, fasten off.

<12 tr3cl, 12 dc, 24 ch-7 sp>

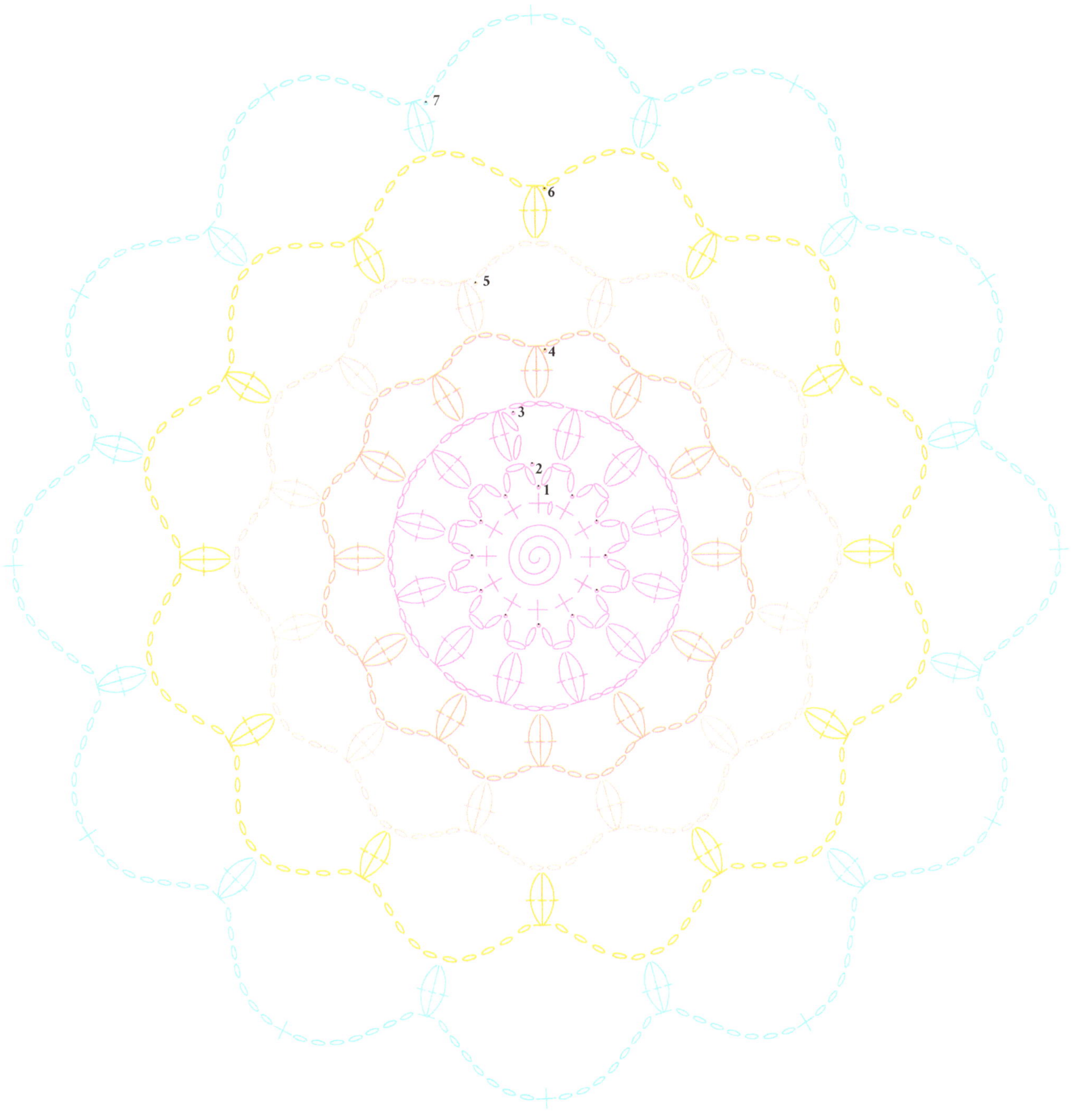

101

OPTIMISM
MANDALA

noun. a disposition or tendency to look on the more favorable side of events or conditions and to expect the most favorable outcome

'Just one more round', said the crocheter with great optimism.

FINISHED SIZE
25cm/9.8in unblocked

MATERIALS
Naturals Organic Cotton
One ball

Colour 1 7200 Blue Dusk

US G-6 / UK 8 / (4mm) hook
Yarn Needle
Scissors

NOTES & TIPS

Project Idea
Jar or bowl cover
Have fun playing with colour and if you are feeling adventurous, you could add beads or turn it into a bowl.

Do not fasten off after each round unless you are playing around with different colours.

Part of being optimistic is keeping one's head pointed toward the sun, one's feet moving forward.

Nelson Mandela

Round 1:
Make a MR, or (ch 4, join to first ch to form ring), beg dtr2cl, ch 3, (dtr2cl, ch 3) 7 times in ring, join to top of beg dtr2cl, do not faten off. *<8 dtr2cl, 8 ch-3 sp>*

Round 2:
Ch 1 (doesn't count as st here and throughout), dc in same st as join, 3 dc in ch-3 sp, [dc in next st, 3 dc in ch-3 sp] around, join to first dc made, do not fasten off. *<32 dc>*

Round 3:
Beg dtr2cl in same st as join, ch 3, sk st, dc in next st, ch 3, sk st, [dtr2cl in next st, ch 3, sk st, dc in next st, ch 3, sk st] around, join to first cl made, do not fasten off.
<8 dtr2cl, 8 dc, 16 ch-3 sp>

Round 4: *This round is worked only in dtr2cl sts from previous round*
Ch 1, [3 dc in same dtr2cl st, ch 5] around, join to first dc made, do not fasten off.
<24 dc, 8 ch-5 sp>

Round 5:
Ch 1, dc in same st as join, dc in next 2 sts, 5 dc in ch-5 sp, [dc in next 3 sts, 5 dc in ch-5 sp] around, join to first dc made, do not fasten off. *<64 dc>*

Round 6:
Sl st to next dc, beg dtr2cl in same st as join, ch 3, sk st, dc in next, ch 3, sk st, [dtr2cl in next, ch 3, sk st, dc in next, ch 3, sk st] around, join to first cl made, do not fasten off. *<16 dtr2cl, 16 dc, 32 ch-3 sp>*

Round 7: *This round is worked only in dtr-2cl sts from previous round*
(Beg dtr2cl, ch 7, dtr2cl) in same st, (dtr2cl, ch 7, dtr2cl) in each st around, join to first cl made, do not fasten off.
<32 dtr2cl, 16 ch-7 sp>

Round 8:
Ch 1, dc in same st as join, (ch 3, dtr3cl, ch 3, dtr3cl) in ch-7 sp, ch 3, sk dtr2cl, [dc in next dtr2cl, (ch 3, dtr3cl, ch 3, dtr3cl) in ch-7 sp, ch 3, sk dtr2cl] around, join to first dc made, do not fasten off. *<32 dc, 32 dtr3cl, 48 ch-3 sp>*

Round 9:
Ch 1, starting in first first ch-3 sp made, [3 dc in ch-3 sp, dc in st, (3 dc, picot 5, 3 dc) in ch-3 sp, dc in st, 3 dc in ch-3 sp, sk st] around, join to first dc made, fasten off.
<224 dc, 16 picot 5>

ORIGINALITY
MANDALA

noun. ability to think or express oneself in an independent and individual manner; creative ability.
As long as you like or love your project, that's all that matters. It's yours. Original. You.

FINISHED SIZE
25cm/9.8in unblocked

MATERIALS
Naturals Organic Cotton
One ball

Colour 1 7196 Sage

US G-6 / UK 8 / (4mm) hook

Yarn Needle

Scissors

NOTES & TIPS
Project Idea
Coaster or small wall hanging

Do not fasten off after each round unless you are playing around with different colours.

It is better to fail in originality than to succeed in imitation.

Herman Melville

Round 1:
Make a MR, or (ch 4, join to first ch to form ring), beg dtr2cl, ch 3, (dtr2cl, ch 3) 7 times, join to top of beg dtr2cl, do not fasten off. *<8 dtr2cl, 8 ch-3 sp>*

Round 2:
Ch 1 (doesn't count as st here and throughout), dc in same st as join, 3 dc in ch-3 sp, [dc in next st, 3 dc in ch-3 sp] around, join to first dc made, do not fasten off. *<32 dc>*

Round 3:
Beg dtr2cl in same st as join, ch 4, sk st, dc in next st, ch 4, sk st, [dtr2cl in next st, ch 4, sk st, dc in next st, ch 4, sk st] around, join to first dtr2cl made, do not fasten off.
<8 dtr2cl, 8 dc, 16 ch-4 sp>

Round 4: This round is worked only in dtr2cl sts from previous round.
Ch 1, 3 dc in same dtr2cl st, ch 5, [3 dc in next cl, ch 5] around, join to first dc made, do not fasten off. *<24 dc, 8 ch-5 sp>*

Round 5:
Ch 1, dc in same st as join, dc in next 2 sts, 5 dc in ch-5 sp, [dc in next 3 sts, 5 dc in ch-5 sp] around, join to first dc made, do not fasten off. *<64 dc>*

Round 6:
Sl st to next st, beg dtr2cl, ch 3, sk st, dc in next, ch 5, sk 3 sts, dc in next, ch 3, sk st, [dtr2cl in next st, ch 3, sk st, dc in next st, ch 5, sk 3 sts, dc in next st, ch 3, sk st] around, join to first dtr2cl made, do not fasten off.
<8 dtr2cl, 16 dc, 8 ch-5 sp, 16 ch-3 sp>

Round 7:
Ch 1, [(dc, ch 2, dc) in dtr2cl st, 3 dc in ch-3 sp, sk st, 5 dc in ch-5 sp, sk st, 3 dc in ch-3 sp] around, join to first dc made, fasten off.
<104 dc, 8 ch-2 sp>

PATIENCE
MANDALA

noun. quiet, steady perseverance; even-tempered care; diligence

Crocheters are filled with patience. Because they don't want to frog, ever.

FINISHED SIZE
17cm/6.7in unblocked

MATERIALS
Naturals Organic Cotton
One ball of each

Colour 1 7174 Buttermilk
Colour 2 7180 Coral
Colour 3 7169 Fondant
Colour 4 7184 Mauve
Colour 5 7195 Faded Denim
Colour 6 7197 Blue Lagoon
Colour 7 7172 Peppermint

US G-6 / UK 8 / (4mm) hook
Yarn Needle
Scissors

NOTES & TIPS
Round 8
Pay attention to where the htr stitches are placed. Don't make a boo-boo and forget to skip the dc stitches.

Have patience with all things, but first of all with yourself.

Saint Francis de Sales

Round 1: C1

Make a MR, or (ch 4, join to first ch to form ring), ch 3 (counts as tr), 11 tr in ring, join to top of ch-3, do not fasten off. *<12 tr>*

Round 2: C1

Sl st to next st, beg dtr3cl, ch 2, dtr in next st, ch 2, [dtr3cl in next st, ch 2, dtr in next st, ch 2] around, join to first cl, fasten off. *<6 dtr3cl, 6 dtr, 12 ch-2 sp>*

Round 3: C2

In any cl, make a standing [dc in dtr3cl, 3 dc in ch-2 sp, dc in dtr, 3 dc in ch-2 sp] around, join to first dc made, fasten off. *<48 dc>*

Round 4: C3

In any dc in cl, make a standing [tr2cl, ch 2, sk st] around, join to first cl made, fasten off. *<24 tr2cl, 24 ch-2 sp>*

Round: 5 C2

In first cl made in prev rnd, make a standing [dc in st, 2 dc in ch-2 sp] around, join to first dc made, fasten off. *<72 dc>*

Round 6: C1

In first st made in prev rnd, make a standing [(tr, ch 2, tr) in st, sk 2 sts] around, join to first tr made, fasten off. *<24 tr, 24 ch-2 sp>*

Round 7: C3:

In first ch-2 sp made, make a standing [7 tr in v st, sk 2 sts, dc in next v st, sk 2 sts] around, join to first tr made, fasten off. *<84 tr, 12 dc>*

Round 8: C2 - *Work htr sts only in 3rd loop*

Make a standing [fpdc around dc, (htr in next st, 2 htr in next st) three times, htr in next st] around, join to first fpdc made. Fasten off. *<12 fpdc, 120 htr in 3rd loop>*

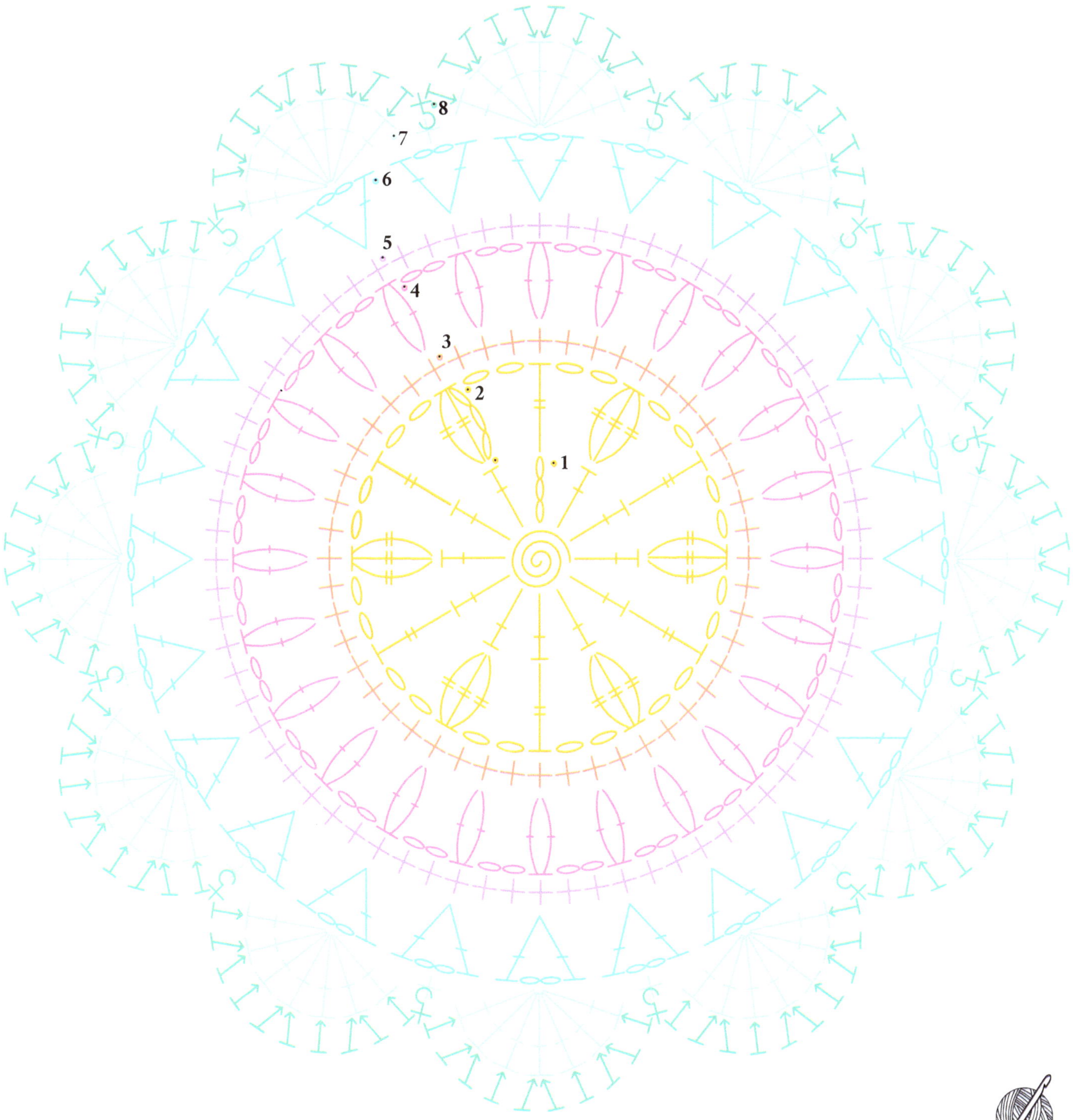

113

PEACE
MANDALA

noun. freedom of the mind from annoyance, distraction, anxiety, an obsession, etc.
If that ufo is annoying you for all the wrong reasons, get rid of it, be at peace with your decision.

FINISHED SIZE
46cm/18.11in unblocked

MATERIALS
Special DK
One ball

Colour 1 1116 Green

US G-7 / UK 7 / (4.5mm) hook
Yarn Needle
Scissors

NOTES & TIPS
Blocking
If you make this mandala with a stretchy yarn such as an acrylic, it will need blocking.

Do not fasten off after each round unless you are playing around with different colours.

If you cannot find peace within yourself, you will never find it anywhere else.

Marvin Gaye

Round 1:
Make a MR, or (ch 6, join to first ch to form ring), ch 1 (doesn't count as st here and throughout), 12 dc in ring, join to first dc made, do not fasten off. *<12 dc>*

Round 2:
Beg tr2cl in same st as join, ch 2, (tr2cl, ch 2) in each st around, join to first cl made, do not fasten off. *<12 tr2cl, 12 ch-2 sp>*

Round 3:
Ch 1, 3 dc in each ch-2 sp around, join to first dc made, do not fasten off. *<36 dc>*

Round 4:
Ch 5 (counts as tr + ch 2 here and throughout), tr in same st as join, ch 1, sk 2 sts, [(tr, ch 2, tr) in next st, ch 1, sk 2 sts] around, join to third ch made, do not fasten off.
<24 tr, 12 ch-2 sp, 12 ch-1 sp>

Round 5:
Sl st to ch-2 sp, (ch 5, tr) in same sp, ch 1, sk st, dc in ch-1 sp, ch 1, sk st, [(tr, ch 2, tr) in next ch-2 sp, ch 1, sk st, dc in next ch-1 sp, ch 1, sk st] around, join to third ch made, do not fasten off.
<24 tr, 12 dc, 12 ch-2 sp, 24 ch-1 sp>

Round 6:
Sl st to ch-2 sp, ch 3, (tr, ch 2, 2 tr) in same sp, ch 2, sk 5 sts, [(2 tr, ch 2, 2 tr) in ch-2 sp, ch 2, sk 5 sts] around, join to third ch made, do not fasten off.
<48 tr, 24 ch-2 sp>

Round 7:
Sl st to ch-2 sp, ch 3 (tr, ch 2, 2 tr) in same sp, ch 1, sk 2 sts, dc in ch-1 sp, ch 1, sk 2 sts, [(2 tr, ch 2, tr) in next ch-2 sp, ch 1, sk 2 sts, dc in ch-2 sp, ch 1, sk 2 sts] around, join to third ch made, do not fasten off.
<48 tr, 24 ch-1 sp, 12 dc, 12 ch-2 sp>

Round 8:
Sl st to ch-2 sp, ch 6 (counts as tr + ch 3 here and throughout), tr in same sp, ch 5, sk 7 sts, [(tr, ch 3, tr) in ch-2 sp, ch 5, sk 7 sts] around, join to third ch made, do not fasten off.
<24 tr, 12 ch-3 sp, 12 ch-5 sp>

Round 9:
Ch 1, dc in same st as join, 3 dc in ch-3 sp, dc in st, 5 dc in ch-5 sp, [dc in st, 3 dc in ch-3 sp, dc in st, 5 dc in ch-5 sp] around, join to first dc made, do not fasten off. *<120 dc>*

Round 10:
Sl st to middle dc of first 2-dc grouping, ch 5, tr in same st, ch 2, sk 4 sts, [(tr, ch 2, tr) in next st, ch 2, sk 4 sts] around, join to third ch made, do not fasten off. *<48 tr, 48 ch-2 sp>*

Round 11:
Sl st to ch-2 sp, (ch 5, tr) in same sp, ch 2, sk st, dc in ch-2 sp, ch 2, sk st [(tr, ch 2, tr) in next ch-2 sp, ch 2, sk st, dc in ch-2 sp, ch 2, sk st] around, join to third ch made, do not fasten off. *<48 tr, 24 dc, 72 ch-2 sp>*

Round 12:
Sl st to ch-2 sp, ch 3, (tr, ch 2, 2 tr) in same

sp, ch 2, sk 7 sts, [(2 tr, ch 2, 2 tr) in next ch-2 sp, ch 2, sk 7 sts] around, join to third ch made, do not fasten off.

<96 tr, 48 ch-2 sp>

Round 13:

Sl st to ch-2 sp, ch 3, (tr, ch 2, 2 tr) in same sp, ch 2, sk 2 sts, dc in ch-2 sp, ch 2, sk 2 sts, [(2 tr, ch 2, 2 tr) in ch-2 sp, ch 2, sk 2 sts, dc in ch-2 sp, ch 2, sk 2 sts] around, join to third ch made, do not fasten off.

<96 tr, 72 ch-2 sp, 24 dc>

Round 14:

Sl st to ch-2 sp, ch 6, tr in same sp, ch 3, sk 9 sts, [(tr, ch 3, tr) in next ch-2 sp, ch 3, sk 9 sts] around, join to third ch made, do not fasten off. *<48 tr, 48 ch-3 sp>*

Round 15:

Ch 1, dc in same st as join, 3 dc in ch-3 sp, [dc in st, 3 dc in ch-3 sp] around, join to first dc made, do not fasten off. *<192 dc>*

Round 16:

Sl st to middle dc, ch 5, tr in same st, ch 1, sk 3 sts, [(tr, ch 2, tr) in next st, ch 1, sk 3 sts] around, join to third ch made, do not fasten off. *<96 tr, 48 ch-2 sp, 48 ch-1 sp>*

Round 17:

Sl st to ch-2 sp, (ch 5, tr) in same sp, ch 1, sk st, dc in ch-1 sp, ch 1, sk st, [(tr, ch 2, tr) in next ch-2 sp, ch 1, sk st, dc in ch-1 sp, ch 1, sk st] around, join to third ch made, do not fasten off. *<96 tr, 48 dc, 96 ch-1 sp, 48 ch-2 sp>*

Round 18:

Sl st to ch-2 sp, ch 3, (tr, ch 2, 2 tr) in same sp, ch 1, sk 5 sts, [(2 tr, ch 2, 2 tr) in ch-2 sp, ch 1, sk 5 sts] around, join to third ch made, do not fasten off.

<192 tr, 48 ch-2 sp, 48 ch-1 sp>

Round 19: *This round will ruffle slightly. A nice block or attaching to ring will flatten it.*

Sl st to ch-2 sp, ch 3 (tr, ch 2, 2 tr) in same sp, ch 1, sk 2 sts, dc in ch-1 sp, ch 1, sk 2 sts, [(2 tr, ch 2, 2 tr) in next ch-2 sp, ch 1, sk 2 sts, dc in ch-1 sp, ch 1, sk 2 sts] around, join to third ch made, fasten off. *<192 tr, 48 dc, 48 ch-2 sp, 96 ch-1 sp>*

PEACE
MANDALA

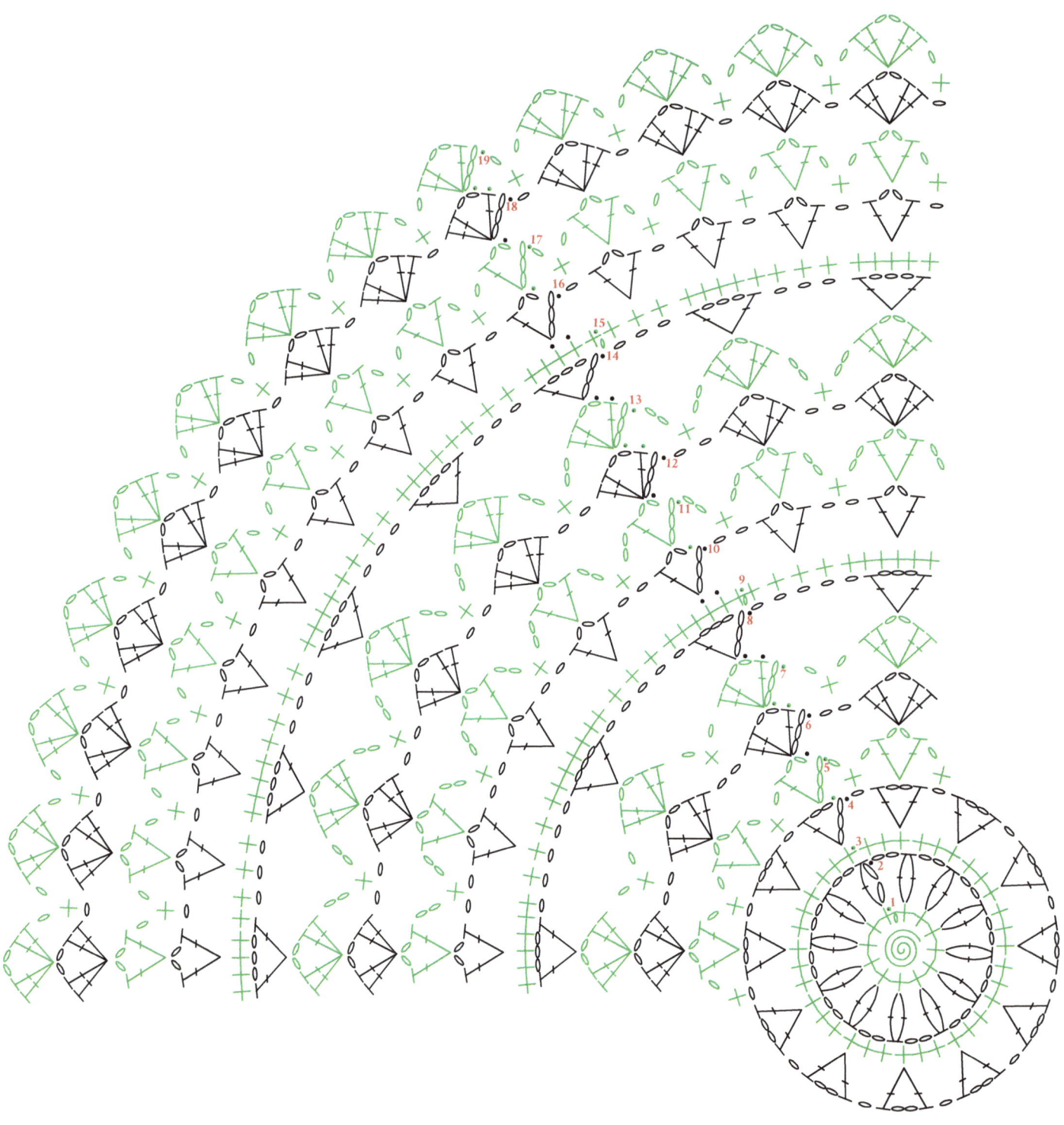

SINCERITY
MANDALA

noun. freedom from deceit, hypocrisy, or duplicity; honesty in intention or in communicating

There is nothing but sincerity when it comes to yourself crocheting, there are no shortcuts. It just is.

FINISHED SIZE

14cm/5.5in unblocked

MATERIALS

Naturals Organic Cotton
One ball of each

Colour 1 7177 Blush
Colour 2 7169 Fondant
Colour 3 7184 Mauve
Colour 4 7172 Peppermint

US G-6 / UK 8 / (4mm) hook
Yarn Needle
Scissors

NOTES & TIPS

Hearts

Can you spot the little hearts in this pattern? How many can you see?

Sincerity means that the appearance and the reality are exactly the same.

Oswald Chambers

Round 1: C1

Make a MR, or (ch 4, join to first ch to form ring), ch 3 (counts as tr), 11 tr in ring, join to 3rd ch made, fasten off. *<12 tr>*

Round 2: C2

In any st, make a standing (tr, puff 3) in each st, join to first tr made, fasten off. *<12 tr, 12 puff 3>*

Round 3: C3

In any tr, make a standing [dc in tr, (fptr, ch 1, fptr) around puff] around, join to first dc made, fasten off. *<12 dc, 24 fptr, 12 ch-1 sp>*

Round 4: C4

In any tr from Rnd 2, make a standing [fptr around tr from Rnd 2, sk st, (htr, tr, ch 2, tr, htr) in ch-1 sp from Rnd 3, sk st] around, join to first fptr made, fasten off.

<12 fptr, 24 tr, 24 htr, 12 ch-2 sp>

Round 5: C1 - *This round may be slightly ruffled but will flatten with following rounds.*

In any ch-2 sp, make a standing [2 dc in ch-2 sp, sk 2 sts, (puff 3, ch 1, puff 3), in fptr, sk 2 sts] around, join to first dc made, fasten off. *<24 puff 3, 24 dc, 12 ch-1 sp>*

Round 6: C2 - *This round will still be slightly ruffled*

In any first dc made after a puff 3, make a standing [2 blo tr in each of next 2 dc sts, sk st, 2 puff 3 in ch-1 sp, sk st] around, join to first blo tr made, fasten off. *<24 puff 3, 48 blo tr>*

Round 7: C3

In any first puff 3 made, make a standing [blo dc in each puff 3 st, blo dc in next tr, fpdtr2tog around puff 3 from Rnd 5 below dc just made and next puff 3 from Rnd 5, sk 2 sts on Rnd 6, blo dc in next tr] around, join to first blo dc made, fasten off. *<48 blo dc, 12 fpdtr2tog>*

Round 8: C4

Around any fpdtr2tog, make a standing [fphtr around fpdtr2tog, blo htr in next 4 sts] around, join to first fphtr made, fasten off. *<12 fphtr, 48 blo htr>*

STRENGTH
MANDALA

noun. mental power, force, or vigor

If you ever see a crocheter walk out of a craft store with nothing, you have witnessed sheer strength.

FINISHED SIZE
17cm/6.7in unblocked

MATERIALS

Naturals Organic Cotton
One ball of each

Colour 1 7187 Flax
Colour 2 7188 Wood
Colour 3 7189 Rosewood
Colour 4 7186 Plum
Colour 5 7175 Citron
Colour 6 7193 Artichoke
Colour 7 7200 Blue Dusk

US G-6 / UK 8 / (4mm) hook
Yarn Needle
Scissors
Stitch Marker

NOTES & TIPS

Round 10
Make sure you make the fp st around both ch-5 sts together.

A calm mind brings inner strength and self-confidence

Dalai Lama

Round 1: C1
Make a MR, or (ch 8, join to first ch to form ring), ch 1 (doesn't count as st), 16 dc in ring, do not fasten off. <16 dc>

Round 2: C1
Ch 4 (counts as tr + ch 1), (tr, ch 1) in each st around, join to third ch made, fasten off. <16 tr, 16 ch-1 sp>

Round 3: C2
In any ch-1 sp, make a standing [tr in ch-1 sp, bptr around st] around, join to first tr made, fasten off. <16 tr, 16 bptr>

Round 4: C3
In any st, make a standing (puff 3, ch 1) in each st around, join to first puff made, fasten off. <32 puff 3, 32 ch-1 sp>

Round 5: C4
In any ch-1 sp, make a standing [2 tr in ch-1 sp, sk puff 3] around, join to first tr made, fasten off. <64 tr>

Round 6: C5
In first tr made in prev rnd, make blo dc in st, blo dc in next 3 sts, [fpdtr2tog around puff before puff below, skip below puff and finish fpdtr2tog around next puff, blo dc in next 4 sts] around, join to first blo dc made, fasten off. Place marker in first fpdtr2tog made. <16 fpdtr2tog, 64 blo dc>

Round 7: C6
In st marker, make [pop in fpdtr2tog, ch 1, blo dc in next 4 sts, ch 1] around, join to first pop made, fasten off. Place st marker in first dc after pop. <64 blo dc, 16 pop, 32 ch-1 sp>

Round 8: C7
In st marker, tr dec over next 2 sts, ch 1, tr dec over next 2 sts, ch 2, sk pop, [tr dec over next 2 sts, ch 1, tr dec over next 2 sts, ch 2, sk pop] around, join to first tr dec made, fasten off. <32 tr dec, 16 ch-1 sp, 16 ch-2 sp>

Round 9: C1
[3 tr in ch-2 sp, ch 5, sk tr dec, flo dc in middle 2 dc from Rnd 6, ch 5, sk tr dec] around, join to first tr made, fasten off. Place st marker in first tr made. <32 flo dc, 48 tr, 32 ch-5 sp>

Round 10: C2
In st marker, make [blo tr in each of next 3 tr, tr in ch-sp, fptr around both ch-5 loops together, tr in ch-sp] around, join to first blo tr made, fasten off. Place st marker in first fptr made. <32 tr, 48 blo tr, 16 fptr>

Round 11: C3
In st marker, make [(puff 3, ch 1, puff 3) in fptr, ch 3, sk 2 sts, dc in next st, ch 3, sk 2 sts] around, join to first puff made, fasten off. Place st marker in last dc made. <32 puff 3, 32 dc, 16 ch-1 sp, 32 ch-3 sp>

Round 12: C4 - *This round may be slightly ruffled but will flatten out with following rounds*
In st marker, make [fpdc around dc, 3 htr in ch-3 sp, htr in st, 2 htr in ch-1 sp, htr in

st, 3 htr in ch-3 sp] around, join to first fpdc made, fasten off. Place st marker in 2nd htr made. *<160 htr, 16 fpdc>*

Round 13: C5

In st marker, make a standing [blo dtr, blo tr in each of next 6 sts, blo dtr in next st, sk 3 sts] around, join to first blo dtr made, fasten off. Place st marker in first blo dtr made. *<32 blo dtr, 96 blo tr>*

Round 14: C7

In st marker, make a standing [puff 3, ch 2, sk st] around, join to first puff 3 made, fasten off. Place st marker in first puff made.

<64 puff 3, 64 ch-2 sp>

Round 15: C1

In st marker, make a standing [dc in puff 3, dtr in unworked st from Rnd 13] around, join to first dc, fasten off. Place st marker in first dc made. *<64 dtr, 64 dc>*

Round 16: C2 – This round is worked in back and third loops only

In st marker, make a standing [2 blo tr in st, blo tr in each of next 7 sts] around, join to first blo tr made, fasten off. Place st marker in first tr made. *<144 blo tr>*

Round 17: C3

In st marker, make a dc, dc in next st, picot 3, [dc in each of next 3 sts, picot 3] around, on final repeat, make dc in last st, join to first dc made, fasten off. Place st marker in first dc made. *<144 dc, 48 picot 3>*

Round 18: C4

In st marker, make a standing [tr2cl, ch 3, sk st, sk picot, sk st] around, join to first tr2cl made, fasten off. Place st marker in first ch-3 sp made. *<48 tr2cl, 48 ch-3 sp>*

Round 19: C5

In st marker sp, make a [(dtr, ch 1) 5 times in ch-3 sp, dtr in same sp, sk st, dc in next ch-3 sp, sk st] around, join to first dtr made, fasten off. *<144 dtr, 120 ch-1 sp, 24 dc>*

STRENGTH
MANDALA

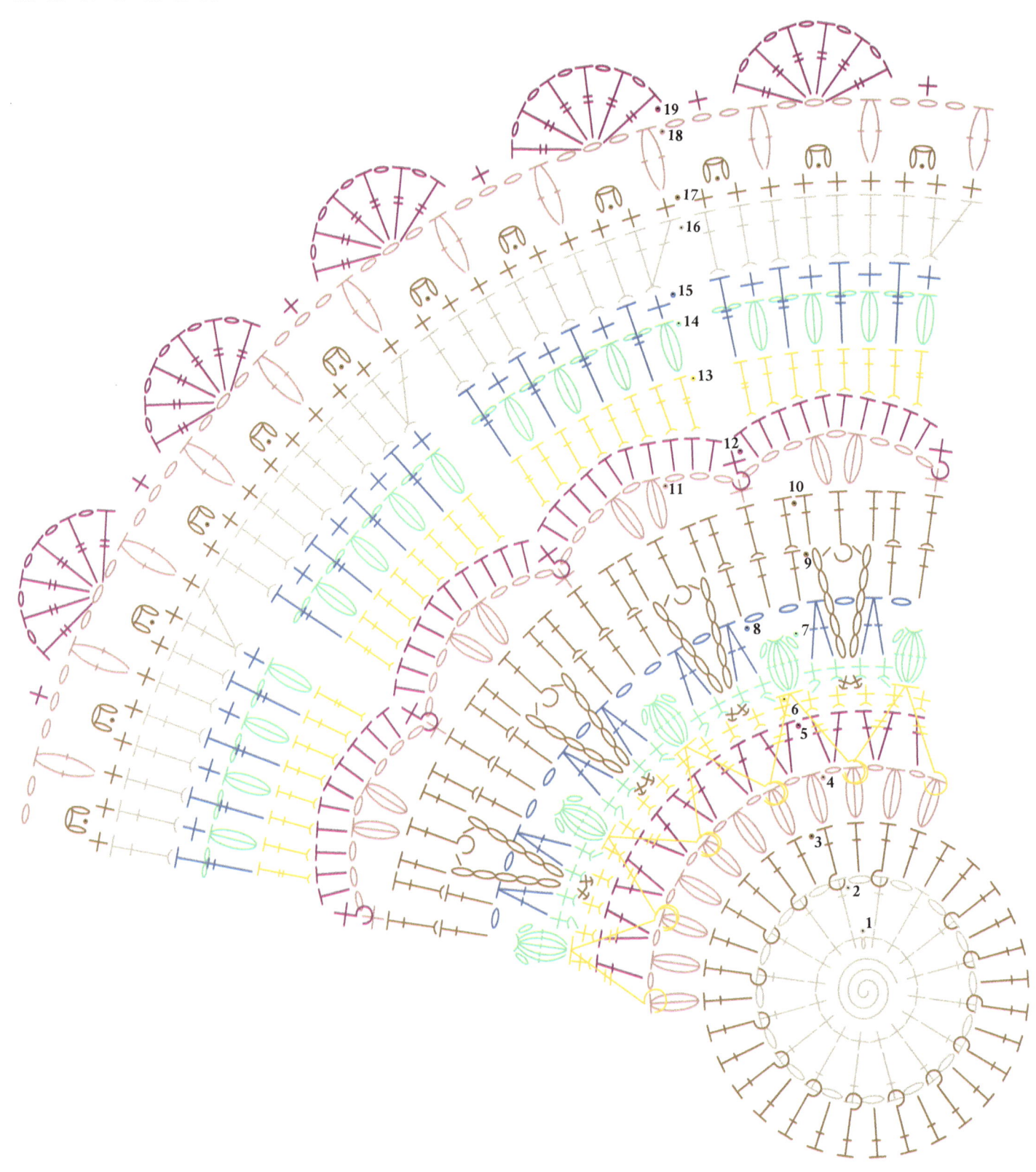

128

TRUSTWORTHY
MANDALA

adjective. deserving of trust or confidence; dependable; reliable

Trustworthy is the fellow crocheter who will stop talking to you while you are counting.

FINISHED SIZE
31cm/12.2in unblocked

MATERIALS

Naturals Organic Cotton
One ball of each

Colour 1 7179 Flamingo
Colour 2 7185 Amethyst
Colour 3 7198 Azure
Colour 4 7192 Sea Green
Colour 5 7191 Jade
Colour 6 7171 Leaf

US G-6 / UK 8 / (4mm) hook
Yarn Needle
Scissors
Stitch Marker
3mm Beads see below

NOTES & TIPS

Beads required

Round 2: 10 Beads
Round 3: 10 Beads
Round 6: 30 Beads
Round 8: 30 Beads
Round 10: 15 Beads
Round 11: 15 Beads

Feel free to complement (match) or contrast (opposite) the colours in your rounds with the beads.

He who does not trust enough will not be trusted.

Lao Tzu

Round 1: C1

Make a MR, or (ch 5, join to first ch to form ring), ch 1 (doesn't count as st), 10 dc in ring, join to first dc made, do not fasten off.

<10 dc>

Round 2: C1

Make a beg dtr3cl, ch 1, IB, ch 1, (dtr3cl, ch 1, IB, ch 1) in each st around, join to first cl made, fasten off.

<10 dtr3cl, 20 ch-1 sp, 10 beads>

Round 3: C2

In ch-1 sp before bead, make a standing [2 tr in ch-1 sp, ch 1, sk bead, 2 tr in ch-1 sp after bead, ch 1, IB, sk cl, ch 1] around, join to first tr made, fasten off.

<40 tr, 30 ch-1 sp, 10 beads>

Round 4: C3

In ch-1 sp between tr pairs (not one with a bead), make a standing [puff 5 in ch-1 sp above bead from Rnd 2, ch 1, sk 2 sts, tr in next ch-1 sp, ch 1, skip bead, tr in next ch-1 sp, ch 1, sk 2 sts] around, join to first puff 5 made, do not fasten off. *<10 puff 5, 20 tr, 30 ch-1 sp>*

Round 5: C3 – *This round may be slightly ruffled*

Ch 3 (counts as tr here and throughout), 2 tr in ch-1 sp, [tr in next st, 2 tr in ch-1 sp] around, join to 3rd ch made, do not fasten off. *<90 tr>*

Round 6: C3

Ch 5 (counts as dtr + ch 1), IB, ch 1, sk 2 sts, [dtr in next st, ch 1, IB, ch 1, sk 2 sts] around, join to 4th ch made, do not fasten off. *<30 beads, 60 ch-1 sp, 30 dtr>*

Round 7: C3 – *This may still be slightly ruffled*

Ch 3, tr in ch-1 sp, sk bead, tr in ch-1 sp, [tr in st, tr in ch-1 sp, sk bead, tr in ch-1 sp] around, join to 3rd ch made, fasten off. *<90 tr>*

Round 8: C4

In a tr in a dtr from Rnd 6, make a standing [tr3cl in middle tr, ch 1, IB, ch 1, sk 2 sts] around, join to first tr3cl made, do not fasten off. *<30 tr3cl, 30 beads, 60 ch-1 sp>*

Round 9: C4

Ch 7, sl st in same st, ch 4, sk ch sts and bead, dc in next cl, ch 4, sk ch sts and bead, [sl st, ch 7, sl st) in cl, ch 4, sk ch sts and bead, dc in next cl, ch 4, sk ch sts and bead] around, join to first cl, fasten off. *<15 ch-7, 30 ch-4 sp, 15 dc>*

Round 10: C5

In any ch-7 loop, make a standing [(7 dtr, ch 1, IB, ch 1, 7 dtr, in ch-7 sp, sl st in dc] around, join to first dtr made, fasten off. *<210 dtr, 15 beads, 30 ch-1 sp, 15 dc, 30 sl st>*

Round 11: C6

Make a standing [fpdc around dc from Rnd 9, bphtr next 7 dtr, htr in ch-1 sp, ch 2, IB, ch 2, sl st in first ch st before bead, sk bead, htr in ch-1 sp, bphtr around next 7 dtr] around, join to first fpdc made, fasten off. *<15 fpdc, 255 bphtr, 30 htr, 15 beads, 60 ch-2 sp>*

133

GLOSSARY

Abbreviations

MR	magic ring	
st/s	stitch/es	
sp/s	space/s	
prev	previous	
rnd/s	round/s	
yo	yarn over	Wrap yarn from back to front around hook.
	3rd loop	The loop behind the v (is seen by looking at both back and front loops from above)
	standing stitch	Make indicated stitch with either slip knot on hook or without. Finish round with invisible join if using no slip knot.
	invisible join	Complete round, cut yarn, pull tail through. Thread tail onto yarn needle, insert needle from front to back under both top loops of the second stitch made, insert needle into the top of the stitch where the tail came from and pull out of the back of the stitch. Weave in ends.
IB	insert bead	Drop loop from working hook, pick up smaller hook, insert bead onto hook, pick up dropped loop, and pull through bead, drop loop off small hook, swap back to working hook.

Stitches & Techniques

ch	chain	
sl st	slip stitch	
dc	double crochet	Insert hook into stitch or space indicated, yo and draw up a loop, yo and pull through both loops on hook.
fpdc	front post double crochet	Insert hook from front to back to front around post of stitch indicated, yo and draw up a loop, yo and pull through both loops on hook.
blo	back loop only	Make stitch into the back and third loop of stitch indicated.
dc dec	double crochet decrease	Insert hook in stitch or space indicated, yo and draw up a loop, insert hook into next stitch or space indicated, yo and draw up a loop, yo and pull through all three loops on hook.
htr	half treble crochet	Yo once, insert hook into stitch or space indicated, yo and draw up a loop, yo and pull through all three loops on hook.
bphtr	back post half treble crochet	Yo once, insert hook from back to front to back around stitch indicated, yo and draw up a loop, yo and pull through all three loops on hook.
fphtr	front post half treble crochet	Yo once, insert hook from front to back to front around stitch indicated, yo and draw up a loop, yo and pull through all three loops on hook.
tr	treble crochet	Yo once, insert hook into stitch indicated, yo and draw up a loop, (yo and pull through two loops) two times.

GLOSSARY

fptr	front post treble crochet	Yo once, insert hook from front to back to front around stitch indicated, yo and draw up a loop, (yo and pull through two loops) two times.
tr dec	treble crochet decrease	Yo, insert hook into stitch or space indicated, yo and pull up a loop, yo and pull through two loops, yo and insert hook into NEXT stitch or space indicated, yo and pull up a loop, yo and pull through two loops, yo and pull through three loops on hook.
tr3dec	treble crochet 3 decrease	Yo, insert hook into stitch or space indicated, pull up a loop, yo and pull through two loops, [yo, insert hook into next stitch or space indicated, pull up a loop, yo and pull through two loops] two times, yo and pull through four loops on hook.
beg tr2cl	beginning treble crochet 2 cluster	Ch 2 (counts as first part of cluster), yo once, insert hook into stitch or space indicated, yo and draw up a loop, yo and pull through two loops, yo and pull through both loops on hook.
beg tr3cl	beginning treble crochet 3 cluster	Ch 2 (counts as part of cluster), *yo, insert hook into stitch or space indicated, yo and draw up a loop, yo and pull through two loops*, leaving two loops on hook, repeat from * to *, leaving three loops on hook, yo and pull through all three loops on hook.
tr2cl	treble crochet 2 cluster	(Yo once, insert hook into stitch or space indicated, yo and draw up a loop, yo and pull through two loops) twice, yo and pull through all three loops on hook.
tr3cl	double treble 3 cluster	[Yo, insert hook into stitch or space indicated, yo and draw up a loop, yo and pull through two loops] three times, leaving three loops on hook, yo and pull through all loops on hook.
dtr	double treble crochet	Yo twice, insert hook into stitch or space indicated, yo and draw up a loop, (yo and pull through two loops) three times.
fpdtr	front post double treble crochet	Yo twice, insert hook from front to back to front around post of stitch indicated, yo and draw up a loop, (yo and pull through two loops) three times.
beg dtr2cl	beginning double treble 2 cluster	Ch 3 (counts as first part of treble cluster), yo twice, insert hook in stitch or space indicated, yo and draw up a loop, (yo and pull through two loops) twice, leaving two loops on hook, yo and pull through both loops on hook.
dtr2cl	double treble 2 cluster	*Yo twice, insert hook in stitch or space indicated, yo and draw up a loop (yo and pull through two loops) twice*, leaving two loops on hook. Repeat from * to * once and pull through all three loops on hook.
beg dtr3cl	beginning double treble 3 cluster	Ch 3 (counts as the first part of treble cluster), *yo twice, insert hook in stitch or space indicated, yo and draw up a loop, (yo and pull through two loops) two times*, leaving two loops on hook, repeat from * to * once, then yo and pull through all three loops on hook.

GLOSSARY

dtr3cl	double treble 3 cluster	*Yo twice, insert hook in stitch or space indicated, yo and draw up a loop (yo and pull through two loops) two times*, leaving two loops on hook. Repeat from * to * two times then yo and pull through all four loops on hook.
beg dtr4cl	beginning double treble 4 cluster	Ch 3 (counts as first part), [Yo two times, insert hook into stitch or space indicated, yo and pull up a loop, (yo and pull through two loops) two times] three times, yo and pull through all four loops on hook.
dtr4cl	double treble 4 cluster	[Yo two times, insert hook into stitch or space indicated, yo and pull up a loop, (yo and pull through two loops) two times] four times, yo and pull through all five loops on hook.
dtr6cl	double treble 6 cluster	With loop on hook, *yo twice, insert hook into stitch or space indicated, yo and pull up a loop, (yo and pull through two loops) twice*, repeat from * to * two more times on one side of popcorn, repeat from * to * 3 times on other side of popcorn, yo, pull through all seven loops on hook.
fpdtr2tog	front post double treble 2 together	Yo twice, insert hook from front to back to front around stitch indicated, pull up a loop, (yo and pull through two loops) two times, yo twice and insert hook around next stitch indicated, pull up a loop, (yo and pull through two loops) two times, yo and pull through all three loops on hook.
crossover dtr		Work dtr stitch in stitch indicated, ch 1, work next dtr in stitch prev to first tr made, sk unworked st.
pop	popcorn	Work 5 tr into stitch or space indicated, drop loop from hook, insert into first tr made, pick up dropped loop and pull through first st.
puff 3	puff 3	(Yo, insert hook into stitch or space indicated and pull up a loop) three times, yo and pull through six loops, yo and pull through last two loops on hook.
puff 5	puff 5	(Yo, insert hook into stitch or space indicated and pull up a loop) five times, yo and pull through 10 loops, yo and pull through last two loops on hook.
picot 3		Ch 3, slip stitch in front loop and last leg of stitch prior to ch-3 stitches.
picot 5		Ch 5, slip stitch in front loop and last leg of stitch prior to ch-5 stitches.
v st		Make (tr, ch 1, tr) in stitch or space indicated.
fptrtr	front post triple treble crochet	Yo three times, insert hook from front to back to front around indicated stitch, pull up a loop, (yo and pull through two loops) four times.
trtr2cl	triple treble crochet 2 cluster	[Yo three times, insert hook into stitch or space indicated, yo and draw up a loop, (yo and pull through two loops) three times] two times, leaving two loops on hook, yo and pull through all three loops on hook.

GLOSSARY

trtr2cl	triple treble crochet 2 cluster	[Yo three times, insert hook into stitch or space indicated, yo and draw up a loop, (yo and pull through two loops) three times] two times, leaving two loops on hook, yo and pull through all three loops on hook.
fphtr2tog	front post half treble crochet 2 together	Yo, insert hook around stitch indicated from front to back to front, yo and pull up a loop, yo and insert hook around next stitch indicated from front to back to front, yo and pull up a loop, yo and pull through five loops on hook.
x st	x st	With slip knot on hook or working loop on hook, yo twice, insert hook into stitch or space indicated, yo and pull up a loop, yo and pull through two loops, sk st, yo and insert hook into next stitch or space indicated, yo and pull up a loop, (yo and pull through two loops) three times, ch 2, yo and insert hook into 2 middle front loops of stitch just made, yo and pull up a loop, (yo and pull through two loops) two times.

CROCHET HOOK SIZES

METRIC	US	UK/CANADA
2.00mm	-	14
2.25mm	B-1	13
2.50mm	-	12
2.75mm	C-2	-
3.00mm	-	11
3.125mm	D	-
3.25mm	D-3	10
3.50mm	E-4	9
3.75mm	F-5	-
4.00mm	G-6	8
4.25mm	G	-
4.50mm	7	7
5.00mm	H-8	6
5.25mm	I	-
5.50mm	I-9	5
6.00mm	J-10	4
6.50mm	K	3
7.00mm	-	2
8.00mm	L-11	0
9.00mm	M/N-13	00
10.00mm	N/P-15	000

SYMBOLS USED

[ ]   Work instructions within brackets as many times as directed
( )   Work instructions within parentheses in same stitch or space indicated
* *   Repeat the instructions between asterisks as many times as directed
< >   These brackets consist of the stitch count per round.

NOTES

Throughout this book, I use standing stitches to start each round when a new colour is used. This replaces joining with a slip stitch and chaining the appropriate length required. To finish these rounds, I use and recommend invisible joins.

Scan the QR Code to watch a video on how to make Standing Stitches. →

Scan the QR Code to watch a video on how to make Invisible Joins. →

If you are unable to scan the codes, you can find these videos on my YouTube Channel by searching for 'The Loopy Stitch'.

I try to write my patterns so that all skill levels can understand them. That in mind, some may find them trickier, depending on your crochet and pattern reading experience. I would recommend having a go, breaking it down to more smaller manageable pieces and going from there. I do have a Facebook Group where you can also share your pieces made by my patterns, ask for help and connect with other like-minded crocheters. If you search 'The Loopy Stitch CAL (Crochet-Along) Group', you will need to request to join and complete the answers accordingly.

I have also included quotes, definitions and have tried to link each pattern name directly with crochet, just for some fun and a personal touch. These quotes were found on Google and the definitions were found on Dictionary.com.

I'd love to know if you have a favourite saying, quote or mandala. Feel free to send me finished photos, questions, or wip photos to theloopystitches@gmail.com.

As this book has been self-published by myself, a human being, there may be typographical errors. If you do come across anything please let me know by reaching out to the email address above.

HOW TO INSERT BEADS

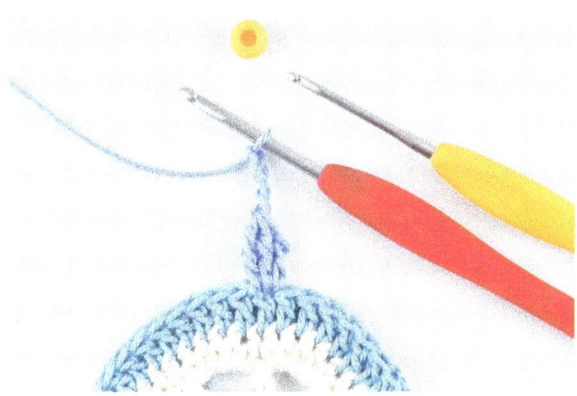

Finish last step in pattern before inserting bead, e.g. last ch st then drop hook from loop.

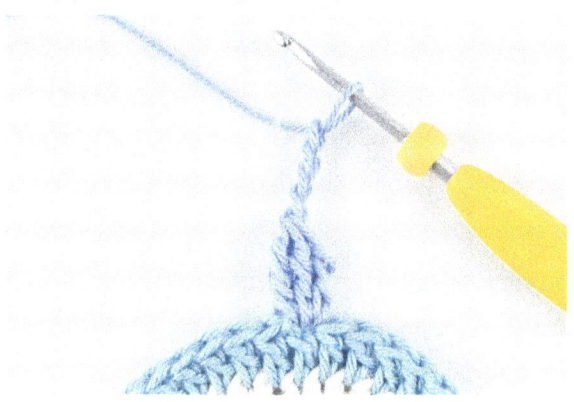

With smaller hook, pick up bead with hook, then pick up dropped loop.

Pull loop through bead.

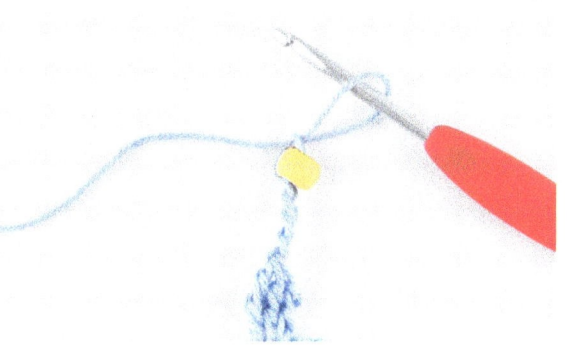

Change back to working hook, make pattern as instructed.

Ta-daa! Pretty beads. It may take a few goes to find what feels natural to you, but you will get it and you will have added something else to your crochet library.

STITCH KEY

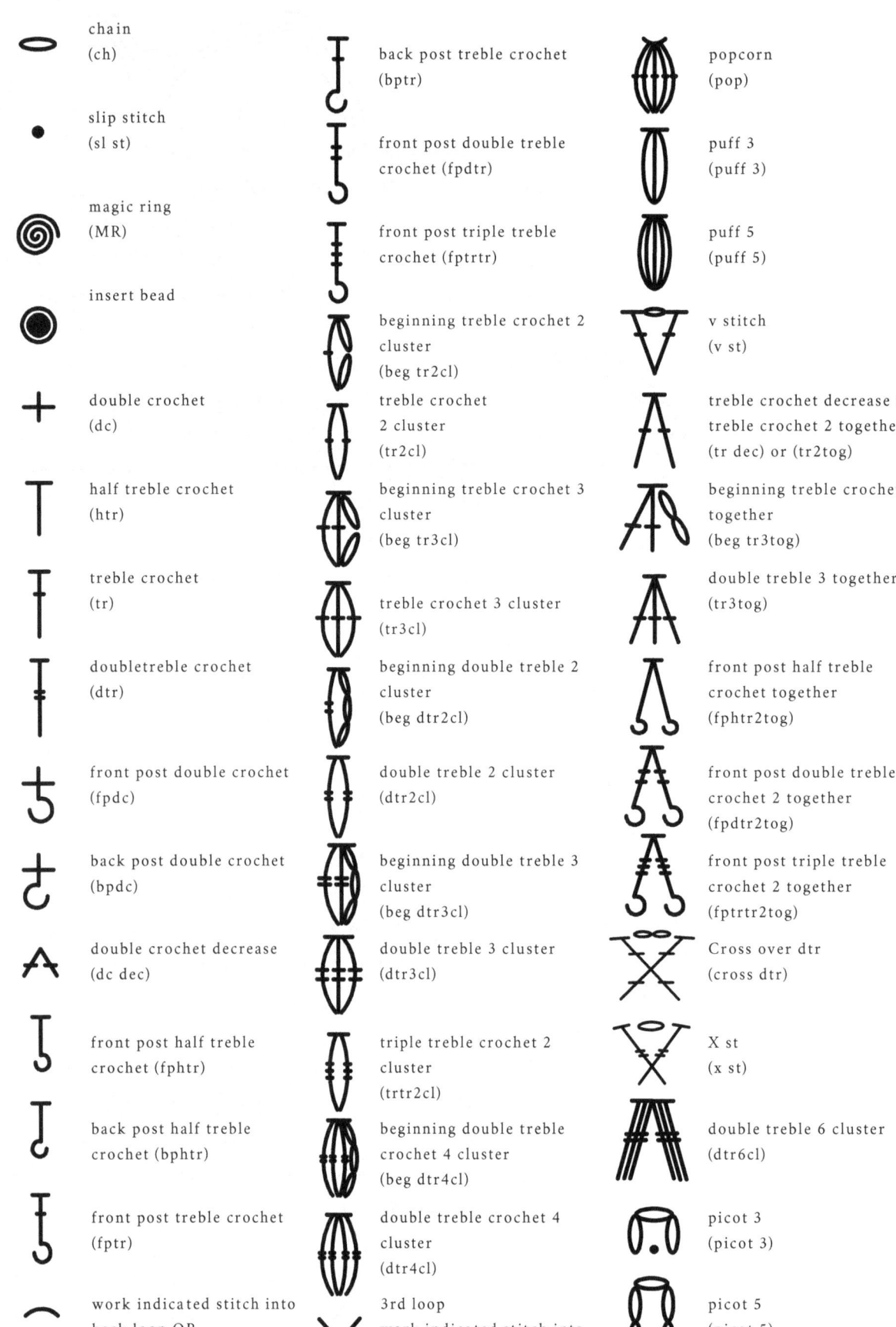

YARN USED

This book is made up exclusively of four types of Stylecraft Yarns: Stylecraft Naturals Organic Cotton; Stylecraft Naturals Bamboo and Cotton; Stylecraft Special Double Knit (DK); Stylecraft Special Aran. The majority of the patterns are made with Organic Cotton, purely as a personal preference because I love how the natural fibres glide effortlessly over the hook.

I have included the overall yarn required for each pattern. Most designs allow for one ball of each colour with ample yarn left over after completion.

Feel free to play around with colours and colour placement, and also the yarn. Please note that I have given approximate sizes using the hooks and yarn mentioned for each pattern.

You will notice I do not mention a gauge when it comes to mandalas. This is due to you, the crocheter maybe wanting to use any yarn, your tension and hook size etc. There are quite a few variables when it comes to gauges and mandalas. But I believe, if you have your yarn that you love and you know the hook that works best with that yarn and want to use that, then go ahead, stick with what you know.

I purchase my Stylecraft Yarn online and usually select the expensive shipping option as regular shipping can take a while to arrive to the land down under, and I'm impatient and want my yarn in my hands and on my hook yesterday. I'm sure a lot of you would be the same.

If you can't access the yarn you need or want to try, I recommend yarnsub.com. This website helps find close matches to the yarn you are searching for. It's a great tool to add to your crochet library. Genius really.

HOOKS

As mentioned above, you will know what hook size works with the yarn you use most often.
Feel free to play around though. If you have never used these types of yarn and notice cupping, go up a hook size. The same as if you're noticing larger than normal gaps and space, try going down a size.

When you make the mandalas that contain beads, you will need a smaller size for inserting the beads. This will depend on the hook and yarn you're using to make the project but mainly the beads. See the previous page for how to insert beads using the method I use in this book. Game changer! No more threading beads on before hand.

I work with five different hook sizes throught this book: 2.5mm; 3.5mm; 4.00mm; 4.50mm and 5.00mm. Hook sizes are stated on each pattern as a guide.

NOTES

MAKING MANDALAS

NOTES

MAKING MANDALAS

NOTES

MAKING MANDALAS